15 Secrets Successful People Know About Time Management

---

*The Productivity Habits of 7 Billionaires,
13 Olympic Athletes, 29 Straight-A Students, and
239 Entrepreneurs*

KEVIN KRUSE
New York Times Bestselling Author

Second Edition

THE KRUSE GROUP

Philadelphia

Double Your Productivity *Without* Feeling Overworked And Overwhelmed!

What if you had an extra hour each day to read, exercise, or to spend with your family?

Based on survey research and interviews with billionaires, Olympic athletes, straight-A students, and over 200 entrepreneurs—including Mark Cuban, Kevin Harrington, James Altucher, John Lee Dumas, Grant Cardone, and Lewis Howes—*New York Times* bestselling author, Kevin Kruse, answers the question:

What are the secrets to extreme productivity?

You will learn:
- How to cure procrastination with "Time Travel"
- How to save 8 hours a week with "3 Questions"
- How to identify your *real* top priorities
- How to get to zero emails in your inbox every day
- How the E-3C system will boost productivity by 10x
- How to reduce stress with the Richard Branson Tool
- How to leave work at 5:00 without feeling guilty
- How to run meetings like Apple, Google & Virgin
- How to conquer social media distractions
- **BONUS**: Discover Your Time Personality quiz
- **BONUS**: 100+ Time Management Quotes

YOUR TWO FREE GIFTS

As a thank you for buying this book, I'm offering two FREE resources:

1) How Millionaires Schedule Their Day (1-Page Planner Tool)

2) 15 Surprising Things Ultra Productive People Do Differently (Quick Guide)

Go To The Link Below To Get Instant Access:
www.MasterYourMinutes.com

Kevin Kruse
New York Times Bestselling Author
Forbes Contributor
Inc 500 Entrepreneur

CONTENTS

"Overworked and Overwhelmed" on a New Jersey Highway

"License and registration!"

5:20 a.m. Dark and cold, pulled over on the shoulder of Route 1 in New Jersey. I had been heading to work.

"Do you know why I pulled you over?"

Why did he have to shout?

"I assume I was speeding," my voice cracked.

"Speeding!" He leaned down until the brim of his hat touched the top of my window. Eye to eye, he said, "You flew up behind me, rode my bumper, swung around and passed me, and kept on going. *I* was doing 65 in the slow lane."

I wish I could say the officer had been driving an unmarked car, but he wasn't. Big white Crown Vic with the light bar on top. Giant blue and yellow "State Police" decals on the doors.

I can't really explain it. I have no memory of coming up on any car, let alone a well-marked cop car.

Apparently, half asleep and thinking of work, I was driving over 80 miles per hour when I came upon a state trooper who was going a measly 65, so I just switched lanes and drove right past him.

"I'm sorry, officer. I just, uh, zoned out I guess…"

"Zoned out?!"

"I didn't get much sleep, and…"

I was lucky he didn't arrest me.

I was really lucky I didn't crash and kill somebody.

This was 20 years ago, when I was young and dumb. I was so "crazy busy" that I just kept adding more hours to my workday and more tasks to each hour. I'd leave the house at five in the morning and work until midnight. No time for proper meals. Coffee and a buttered roll eaten in my car for breakfast. Skipped lunch. Wolfed down dinner standing up.

I drank so many diet Red Bulls that I started looking at those silver and blue cans the way an alcoholic looks at a bottle of wine. Those cans called to me.

Passing a trooper on the highway without even realizing it was definitely the worst thing I did, but there were other signs of being out of control before that.

Like when I filled up my car with gas, drove away, and KLAANK! I had forgotten to take the gas nozzle out of my car. It's a miracle I didn't blow the place up.

And the times my wife kept telling me, "I just don't feel connected to you anymore." She's now my ex-wife.

It wasn't like I was completely clueless about time management. I had read all the bestsellers. I was the master of the to-do list and prioritized it every night for the next day. At one point I had such a long list that I used a standard piece of ruled notebook paper and filled in *two* columns—35 ruled lines, 2 tasks per line, 70 total to-do items.

I look back at that time in my life with horror and embarrassment.

Thankfully, today I'm a different person.

I'm a single dad with three kids. I help them with their homework every night and am home for dinner at the kitchen table more than half the time. I attend most of their games, plays, and music recitals. I'm no athlete, but I exercise routinely and am maintaining a healthy weight. I manage at least one or two "date nights" with my girlfriend each week.

For work, I run a small consulting practice, write two books a year, give speeches around the world, and oversee my investments in various startups and commercial real estate.

I take a lot of vacation time, too. Last year alone I went to Puerto Rico, Cancun, and the Jersey shore; spent several weekends in New York City; and for my daughter's 16th birthday, I took her on an epic trip to Barcelona, Madrid, and to see the running of the bulls in Pamplona.

I do all this—and this is the key point—*while rarely feeling stressed out, rushed, overwhelmed, or guilty*. I definitely don't feel "crazy busy" and don't feel the need to brag about being "crazy busy" to those around me.

Don't you just hate me?

My personal time and stress transformation started as I began to ask my successful friends how *they* managed time.

I immediately noticed that none of them mentioned the things that are taught in traditional time management books.

My curiosity soon turned into a quest, and I did original survey research of working professionals, looking for correlations between specific time management practices and productivity, stress, and happiness. I funded a study of thousands of working professionals and we found no correlation between time management training and higher levels of productivity or reduced stress. Zero!

I then interviewed hundreds of highly successful people including Mark Cuban and other billionaires, famous entrepreneurs, gold medal Olympians like Shannon Miller, and straight-A students.

What I discovered is that highly successful people don't prioritize tasks on a to-do list, or follow some complex five-step system, or refer to logic tree diagrams to make decisions.

Actually, highly successful people don't think about time much at all. Instead, they think about values, priorities, and *consistent habits.*

While no two people manage time exactly the same way, there are common themes. And if you really try them, you might find that just one of their "secrets" has the power to transform your career and your life.

Kevin Kruse
Bucks County, PA

CHAPTER 1

The Power of 1440

Can a single number change your life?

A three-word question used to send chills of dread down my spine.

"Got a minute?"

Sure, I believed in an open door policy. Sure, I was the boss. Sure, some people would say I was overly detail oriented, which made people check in with me too frequently (who, me?).

I was the founder and president of a digital learning company that quickly took off. Revenue doubling every year and all the related challenges: new hires, sales, product launches, fundraising, and on and on.

The fires to put out kept multiplying, as did the knocks on my office door followed by, "Got a minute?"

There was nothing wrong with people asking me for advice or help. But I quickly found entire days were being spent on other people's priorities and problems as the requested minute-meetings inevitably turned into 30 minutes or more. My priorities, the company's strategic priorities—washed away by the never-ending torrent of "urgent" got-a-minutes.

Finally, I printed a big **1440** on a piece of paper and taped it to the outside of my office door.

No other words. No explanation. Just "1440" in Arial, bold, 300-point font.

How I Beat Back Time Thieves

Every time I walked into my own office, I passed that giant "1440" sign as a reminder. Tick, tick, tick. I could not be careless with my minutes.

But what also happened was that when people stopped by to ask, "Got a minute?" and I would say yes, they would immediately ask, "So what's that 1,440 all about?"

I would explain that it was a simple reminder to *me* of the value of time and how I needed to "invest" each minute of my day very wisely.

I always made it about me, but the length of these got-a-minute meetings suddenly got shorter. One person heard my explanation and replied, "You know what, I don't need to talk anymore. I just realized it can wait until the team huddle on Monday."

I can only assume that my 1440 sign initially freaked people out. *Kevin must be in a bad mood; he doesn't want us talking to him anymore. Kevin's a hypocrite...he says he has an open door policy but then insults us with that sign.*

But the sign stayed up, and the novelty wore off. Soon I heard other people in the office talking about "only 1440 minutes" as they prioritized tasks or turned down invitations to irrelevant meetings.

1,440 Minutes in a Day

If you're like most people who want to improve their time management, you probably want a list of tips, tools, and systems that will increase your productivity and add hours to your week.

Yet, the single most important thing when it comes to time and productivity isn't a tactic or a trick—it's a shift in mindset.

Self-made millionaires, professional athletes, straight-A students, and other highly successful people think about time differently. They experience time differently.

In Their Own Words...

Before I decide to take on a new project, I analyze it...How much of my time will this take, and what is my financial upside potential. I create a "dollar per minute" analysis, hopefully a million dollar per week upside.

–Kevin Harrington is the inventor of the infomercial, a bestselling author, an original investor on Shark Tank, and founder and chairman of As Seen On TV, Inc.

Take a minute to think about the most valuable things in life. Really take a minute to look up from this book, maybe even close your eyes, and come up with a list of all the things in the world that you value most.

I'll wait...

Did you really do this little exercise? Don't just read this book and let it go in and out! You need to do the activities to anchor the lessons. Changing behaviors is hard and passively reading won't get it done. Do it!

OK, if you are like most people, your list of the most valuable things includes your spouse, children, friends, health, money, and of course, time.

Highly successful people have a similar list—but they rank time as the most important item of all.

Shouldn't health be number one? You can be healthy, and then get sick, and then regain your health.

How about money? You can lose all your money, and then you can make it all back.

Friends? Friends are important, and yet, how many friends did you have back in college that you no longer keep in touch with? Or even people who were guests at your wedding, and that was the last day you ever saw them? Yes, friends are prized, yet we lose them and make new ones all the time.

Yes, your spouse means the world to you. And 50 percent of married people get a divorce, and many divorced people get a new husband or wife that is suddenly the love of their life.

But time...

You can never lose time and get it back again.

You can't spend time and go earn more of it. You can't buy it, rent it, or borrow it.

Time Is the Most Important Asset

Time is unique because it's the one true equalizer. Some people are born rich, others born poor. Some have Ivy League degrees, while others are high school dropouts. Some are genetically gifted athletes, others physically challenged.

But we all have the same minutes in a day. Time is the lowest common denominator.

Hold your hand to your heart.

Again, I need you to really do it. Hold your hand to your chest and feel your heart. Beat, beat, beat.

Become conscious of your breathing. In. Out. In. Out.

You will never get those beats back. You will never get those breaths back. In fact, I just took three beats away from your life. I just took two breaths from you.

But it was worth it if it helped you to truly feel time slipping away.

You might be thinking, "Yeah, yeah, the importance of time. Of course, that's why I'm reading this. I get it!"

But are you *living* it?

Think about how much attention you give to your money. Working hard to make money, tracking your money in your bank account, researching the best ways to invest your money, reading about ways to make more money, worrying that somebody might steal your money.

You would never leave your wallet sitting out in the open. You'd never give your ATM card and password to a bunch of strangers.

And yet we typically think little about our time. We routinely let people steal our time, even though it's our most valuable possession.

The magic number that can change your life is 1,440.

I encourage you to try it yourself. Just draw a big "1,440" on a piece of paper and tape it on your office door, under your TV, next to your computer monitor—wherever it will best serve as a constant reminder of the very limited and oh so precious time you have each day.

Why Minutes, Not Seconds?

There are 86,400 seconds in a day. And if that number is more powerful to you, by all means, put up a "86,400" sign to remind you of time.

But personally, I find focusing on minutes to be more powerful. Seconds can slip away fairly easily. But minutes! Just think of all the ways you can spend just one minute.

I asked the members of my Facebook page (www.facebook.com/KruseAuthor) how they could use a single minute. Their responses included:

- Do 30 sit-ups
- Tell someone how much you love them
- Do a yoga Breath of Fire
- Write a thank you note
- Introduce yourself to a stranger
- Read a poem
- Have a great idea

- Water a plant
- Pet your cat
- Have your heart broken or break a heart
- Sing a song
- Write in a journal
- Eat an apple
- Drink a glass of water
- Send a text to someone you are thinking about
- Stand in the sun
- Write three things you're grateful for
- Make a decision to give up smoking
- Give feedback
- Give a donation
- Apologize
- Boil water for tea
- Send a positive tweet
- Daydream
- Smile
- Take a photo that will turn into a memory
- Plank
- Breathe…in with abundance, out with gratitude
- Journal
- Hug your mom
- Have one really, really good kiss
- Recall a happy moment
- Meditate
- Pray

Highly successful people feel the passage of time. They know the potential that every minute holds.

In Their Own Words...

I'll just say that actually being disciplined about adopting these habits is, in my experience, a huge differentiator of successful people...If I was building a character in a business video game and I had ten character points to distribute, I'd put three of them into intelligence and seven of them into self-discipline.

−Andrew Mason *is the co-founder of Detour and co-founder and former CEO of Groupon.*

When you wake up and subconsciously start the count-down—1440, 1439, 1438—adopting the habits of highly successful people becomes very easy.

SECRET #1

Time is your most valuable and scarcest resource.

How would your life change if each and every day you truly felt your 1,440 minutes?

* * FREE BONUS * *

To download a ready-to-print "1440" poster and other FREE bonuses, visit: www.MasterYourMinutes.com

CHAPTER 2

The Power of Proper Priorities

How would you like to be totally clear on your "one thing"?

Whose Dreams Are You Chasing Anyway?

If you aren't busy working on your own goals, you'll be working to achieve somebody else's goals.

What's Your One Thing?

In the hilarious 1991 movie *City Slickers*, the old cowboy Curly (played by Jack Palance) gives a secret to Mitch (played by Billy Crystal). Holding up his index finger, Curly explains that you need to figure out your one thing and stick to it.

But the "one thing" concept goes back a lot further than a Billy Crystal comedy. Consider this advice from the ages:

- "To do two things at once is to do neither." –Publilius Syrus
- "If you chase two rabbits, you will catch neither one." –Russian proverb
- "Things which matter most must never be at the mercy of things which matter least." –Goethe

- "It is those who concentrate on but one thing at a time who advance in this world." –Og Mandino
- "Drive for the one thing on which you have decided." –General George Patton
- "Efficiency is doing the thing right. Effectiveness is doing the right thing." –Peter Drucker
- "Success demands singleness of purpose." –Vince Lombardi

Identify Your Most Important Task (MIT)

Therese Macan, a professor at the University of Missouri-St. Louis, conducted groundbreaking research into time management, productivity, and stress, discovering that the two most important keys are priorities and mechanics (i.e., the mechanics of implementing time management techniques and tactics).

Put simply, the most important things are to know *what* to focus on and *how* you are going to get it done. I call this always knowing your *most important task*, or MIT.

Research Says...

In addition to increased productivity, having a daily MIT correlates to higher levels of happiness and energy. (Source: The Kruse Group, 2015)

Entire books have been written on goal setting, and I may write one myself someday, but it all comes down to understanding what is most important to you and what activity right now will provide the greatest leverage to getting there.

In Their Own Words...

About six months before an Olympics, I would relate all the decisions I made to the ultimate vision of winning gold. The simple question I would ask several times a day was, "Will this activity help me perform better and therefore help us win gold?"

*—**Briana Scurry** won two gold medals as the starting goalkeeper for the United States women's soccer team in 1996 and 2004.*

I work more on time alignment. Is this part of my mission? Does this serve others or strengthen my ability to serve others? Those two questions keep me tight to my map. That's how I best manage my time and priorities.

*—**Chris Brogan** is a bestselling author and CEO of Owner Media Group.*

I always start with the most important thing on my priority list. If you didn't spend your week working on the most important thing, it was a week wasted.

*—**Randy Gage** is the author of nine books including the New York Times bestseller, Risky Is the New Safe.*

Most people set goals for health, wealth, and relationships. Others add things like spirituality, charity, and recreation.

Regardless of your focus areas, conventional wisdom dictates that your goal be specific and measurable. Instead of writing a goal to "save money," it should be something like "Save $5,000 by the end of the year." Instead of "lose weight," you would specify, "Lose ten pounds in ten weeks."

After identifying your most important goal, you need to identify which activities will lead to goal achievement and which activity is most important *right now*.

Don't get sidetracked by the goal setting if you don't already have identified goals. In fact, other experts, like CEO coach Peter Bregman, suggest that there is a downside to goals. Instead, Bregman suggests picking focus areas.

For example, at the time I'm writing this book, I know that I really want to increase my passive income this year. But I don't have a specific dollar amount in mind and because I have plenty of money, I'm not feeling any pressure to define it.

But in order to grow passive income, I also know that I need to *create* all kinds of things like books, assessments, and online training. Right now, when I ask myself:

What is the single most important task (MIT) to get closer to my goal right now?

I know it's working on this book. Once the book is done, I'll create spin-off content. And once I have more stuff to sell, my "one thing" will likely be working on marketing material or webinars to spread the word. But for now, I know that my MIT is writing this book.

Your own MIT may look very different based on your job and personal goals. A rookie salesperson's MIT might be cold calling in order to hit a sales target. A software engineer's MIT might be to debug a particular module in order to hit a launch deadline. A senior software executive's MIT might be recruiting a new programmer in order to develop a new app. A startup CEO's MIT might be to create a slide deck in order to land venture capital. A student's MIT might be to find a tutor in order to do well on an upcoming exam. A stay-at-home parent's MIT might be to reserve a campground site at the state park to line up the family's favorite summer vacation.

Mark Pincus on His MIT

Identifying your MIT makes your scheduling decisions much easier. Having identified what is most important to you, you'll need a very good reason *not* to be spending time on it.

The social gaming company Zynga is probably best known for its game *Farmville*, which at its peak had over 265 million active users. Zynga CEO, Mark Pincus, clearly has his MIT well defined and believes in spending at least half of his time on it.

In Their Own Words...

If you want to build great products, devote more than 50 percent of your work hours to product. Don't accept speaking opportunities if you can't justify them as benefitting your users or your company.
–Mark Pincus *is the co-founder and CEO of Zynga.*

Two Awesome Hours in the Morning

After identifying your MIT, you need to turn it into a calendar item and book it as early in your day as possible.

Dan Ariely, a Duke University professor of psychology and behavioral economics, suggests that most people are most productive and have the highest cognitive functioning in the first two hours after they're fully awake. In a Reditt Ask Me Anything, Ariely wrote:

> *One of the saddest mistakes in time management is the propensity of people to spend the two most productive hours of their day on things that don't require high cognitive capacity (like social media). If we could salvage those precious hours, most of us would be much more successful in accomplishing what we truly want.*

Why do we do this? Why do we spend our best hours on our least important tasks?

Many of us jump into our day trying to take care of all the quick and easy things. Responding to all those overnight emails, sorting our stack of mail, signing off on purchase orders…it all feels so productive! *Look, it's only 11:00 in the morning, and I must have done at least 50 things.*

In Their Own Words...

Invest the first part of your day working on your number one priority that will help build your business. Do this without interruptions—no email or text—and before the rest of the world is awake.

—Tom Ziglar *is the CEO of Ziglar, Inc.*

Do creative work first. Reactive work second.

—Jonathan Milligan *is the author of* The 15 Success Traits of Pro Bloggers.

Others choose to do the most unpleasant tasks early in the morning in what's known as the "eat the frog first" strategy.

It's a procrastination-fighting technique that says if you have something unpleasant to do, just get it out of the way first thing. This is good advice if it defeats procrastination, but it can also be counterproductive if you routinely use up your peak hours.

In Their Own Words…

I prepare a MUST DO list the night before…when I get to my desk, I do those items first before I turn on my email.

–Andrew McCauley *is the co-founder of Autopilot Your Business.*

Not only are most people at their cognitive best earlier in the day, but it's less likely that unexpected items will jump onto the calendar or require urgent attention.

In Their Own Words…

I try to reserve the morning for doing "real work." I find I can focus more in the morning whereas it's harder to get focused after having been bombarded by meetings, so I try to save meetings for later in the day.

–Nathan Blecharczyk *is the co-founder of Airbnb.*

Taking Dr. Ariely's advice to heart, drink that first cup of coffee while driving in to work, but then shut your door, silence your phone, close email and social media, and work on your MIT.

In Their Own Words...

I schedule a series of 90-minute "Jam Sessions" throughout my day/week where I focus exclusively on one vital priority and nothing else.

–Stephen Woessner *is host of the Onward Nation podcast and CEO of Predictive ROI.*

I have found that I am most productive from 6:00 a.m. to noon. I'm up, fresh, creative, and that is the time I make crazy things happen. I do more in those hours than people probably do all week.

–Christina Daves *is the author of* PR for Anyone *and the CEO and founder of PR for Anyone®.*

How Does This Apply If You're A(n)...

Entrepreneur: Would it be helpful to identify the one thing that is most important to achieving your quarterly goals?

Executive: Would it be helpful to be crystal clear on the number one objective you'll be evaluated against when it comes time for your annual performance review?

Freelancer: Would it be helpful to identify the one thing that will lead to more clients?

Student: Would it help to pick the one class that is most important for you to raise your grade in?

Stay-at-Home Parent: Would it be helpful to identify the one thing that is currently most important for your child's health and development (e.g., organizing a playgroup, choosing a summer camp, finding a music tutor)?

SECRET #2

Identify your Most Important Task (MIT) and work on it each day before doing anything else.

So, what's your one thing? What's your MIT?

* * FREE BONUS * *

To download the Priorities & MIT worksheet and other FREE bonuses, visit: www.MasterYourMinutes.com

CHAPTER 3

Stop Making To-Do Lists—Do This Instead

Do you really think millionaires and billionaires walk around with a to-do list?

Do you really think Bill Gates, Donald Trump and Warren Buffett write a long to-do list and prioritize items as A1, A2, B1, B2, C1, and on and on?

Do you really think Steve Jobs kept a to-do list and asked himself several times a day, "What's my next action?"

The Problem with To-Do Lists

To-do lists should be called nagging wish-lists. A series of tasks you hope to accomplish, without a specific plan as to when you'll get them all done. How many items on your current to-do list have been on there for several days? For weeks? Months?

The first problem with recording tasks on a to-do list is that it doesn't distinguish between items that take only a few minutes and items that require an hour or more. So when you randomly look at your list and ask, "Hmm, what should I tackle next?" You are very likely going to pick the quick tasks, the easy items, not necessarily the thing that is most important.

Research Says...

*41% of to-do list items are **never** completed.*
(Source: The Busy Person's Guide to the Done List, iDoneThis)

Second, and similar to the first problem, to-do lists make it really easy to work on the *urgent* instead of the important. That's why I still have "Create annual family photo album for 2013" still on my to-do list (from two years ago!). *Do you know how many men have had "colonoscopy" on their to-do list year after year?!*

Research Says...

50% of to-do list items are completed within a day, many within the first hour of being written down.
(Source: The Busy Person's Guide to the Done List, iDoneThis)

Third, to-do lists cause unnecessary stress. Indeed, when we carry around a long list of undone items it's one way to remember them. But it's also a constant reminder, a constant nagging, that there are many things we still need to deal with. No wonder we feel overwhelmed. No wonder at night we collapse exhausted, but fight insomnia as our brain processes all that still has to get done. No wonder our bodies are breaking down from stress.

Research Says...

The Zeigarnik effect is a psychological term based on studies that show unfinished goals cause intrusive, uncontrolled thoughts.

Live Life from Your Calendar

Highly successful people don't have a to-do list, but they do have a very well-kept calendar. One of the most consistent messages I got from all the interviews and research I did for this book was that no matter what it is, if you truly want to get it done, *schedule* time for it.

In Their Own Words...

Use a calendar and schedule your entire day into 15-minute blocks. It sounds like a pain, but this will set you up in the 95th percentile as far as organization goes. If it's not on the calendar, it doesn't get done. If it's on the calendar, it gets done no matter what. Use this not just for appointments, but workouts, calls, email blocks, etc.

*–**Jordan Harbinger** is the co-founder of The Art of Charm and host of The Art of Charm Podcast, a school that teaches networking and relationship-development skills*

This is why hyper-busy politicians, executives and celebrities have full-time schedulers. This is why—as pretentious as it sounds—successful people are prone to saying things like, "Have your people call my people to set something up."

In Their Own Words...

I simply put everything on my schedule. That's it. Everything I do on a day-to-day basis gets put on my schedule. Thirty minutes of social media—on the schedule. Forty-five minutes of email management—on the schedule. Catching up with my virtual team—on the schedule. Quiet time to contemplate and plan—on the schedule. Bottom line, if it doesn't get scheduled, it doesn't get done.

—Chris Ducker is a serial entrepreneur, keynote speaker, and bestselling author as well as a popular business blogger and podcaster.

Surprisingly, the simple act of scheduling tasks on your calendar—instead of writing them on a to-do list—will free your mind, reduce stress, and increase cognitive performance. Florida State University Researchers showed that the Zeigarnik effect—the stressful conscious and unconscious thoughts caused by unfinished tasks—could be overcome simply by making a *plan* to accomplish a task—you didn't actually have to complete the task itself.

Research Says...

*"A **plan** increases one's odds of attaining a goal and simultaneously **reduces cognitive activities**..."*
(Source: Consider It Done!, Journal of Personality and Social Psychology, 2011)

There are several key concepts to managing your life using your calendar instead of a to-do list.

First, schedule a chunk of time for everything that is important to you; this is called "time blocking" or "time boxing." If you truly value being healthy and have decided that a 30-minute daily workout is your enabling goal, then don't put it on your to-do list—put it on your calendar. Schedule it as a recurring appointment. If you value customer intimacy as a business strategy and have an enabling goal of talking to at least two customers a day, then schedule a daily appointment for "customer calls."

In Their Own Words...

During training, I balanced family time, chores, schoolwork, Olympic training, appearances, and other obligations by outlining a very specific schedule. I was forced to prioritize...To this day, I keep a schedule that is almost minute by minute. Focus on those things that bring you further to your goal each and every day. Every moment counts!

*—**Shannon Miller**, a member of the 1992 and 1996 U.S. Olympic gymnastics team who won a combined seven Olympic medals.*

Second, important items should be scheduled as early in the day as possible. No matter how much we try to control our time and calendars, we all have things that "come up" that might need our attention. It could be a meeting request from our boss, an angry client call, or the school nurse calling to say we need to pick up Johnny from school. Naturally, as more time ticks away in each day, the more likely it is that something unexpected will happen.

I personally struggle with this immensely. If I have my daily workout scheduled for the late afternoon or night, the odds are high that I'll feel some other priority is in need of extra attention by the time I actually get to my exercise time block. I basically know that if I don't hit the treadmill in the morning, the odds of hitting it at all go way down.

Third, don't cancel goals; reschedule them if necessary. For example, if you normally work out every day from 12:00 to 1:00 p.m.—during your lunch hour—but you have to be on an airplane on Monday traveling for work at noon, you would reschedule the exercise appointment for earlier or later in the day.

In Their Own Words...

Get one of those big blue calendars. Planning your life on your phone is fine, but it doesn't give you the same perspective.

*—**Will Dean** is an Olympic rower for Canada and competed in the London 2012 Olympics. He is currently training for Rio 2016.*

Fourth, treat your time-blocked calendar entries as if they were appointments with your doctor; they are that important. Most of us cave in on our self-scheduled appointments too easily. If we time block 4:00 to 5:00 p.m. to work on an important report at the office, and then a colleague asks for 15 minutes of time because "something has come up I need to run by you," we reflexively say "sure," thinking we'll finish the report in only 45 minutes, or we'll stay 15 minutes later or adjust in some other way.

But imagine if instead of working on a report you had an appointment with your doctor or dentist. Would you still agree to give away that time and show up for your doctor 15 minutes late? Of course not.

In Their Own Words...

What I found to be the most effective way to manage my time was to buy an agenda with a big calendar. I handwrite what topics I need to cover and how long I need to be studying that topic each night.

*–**Caitlin Hale** was a straight-A student in college and currently attends the University of Medicine and Dentistry of New Jersey.*

If it's not in my calendar, it won't get done. But if it is in my calendar, it will get done. I schedule out every 15 minutes of every day to conduct meetings, review materials, write, and do any activities I need to get done. And while I take meetings with just about anyone who wants to meet with me, I reserve just one hour a week for these "office hours." People can schedule time at http://ScheduleDave.com.

*–**Dave Kerpen** is the NY Times bestselling author of three books, the co-founder & chairman of Likeable Media, and the founder & CEO of Likeable Local.*

The best habit is to automatically respond to unanticipated requests that conflict with your calendar by saying something like, "I have an important appointment on my calendar from 4:00 to 5:00. Is there any chance we can talk after 5:00, or can it wait until the morning?"

You'll be surprised at how frequently the unanticipated item can then be scheduled in an open block. Sure there will be times when an important person—a boss or spouse, for example—needs our attention, and it really is more important than our time block activity. But we can always ask to fit it in elsewhere as a first reaction.

Jeff Weiner Time Blocks Buffer Time

The CEO of LinkedIn, Jeff Weiner, wrote a blog post describing how he time blocks "do nothing" time on his calendar. He wrote:

> *If you were to see my calendar, you'd probably notice a host of time slots greyed out but with no indication of what's going on. There is no problem with my Outlook or printer. The grey sections reflect "buffers," or time periods I've purposely kept clear of meetings.*
>
> *In aggregate, I schedule between 90 minutes and two hours of these buffers every day (broken down into 30- to 90-minute blocks). It's a system I developed over the last several years in response to a schedule that was becoming so jammed with back-to-back meetings that I had little time left to process what was going on around me or just think.*
>
> *At first, these buffers felt like indulgences. I could have been using the time to catch up on meetings I had pushed out or said "no" to. But over time I realized not only were these breaks important, they were absolutely necessary in order for me to do my job.*

Design Your Ideal Week with Time Blocks

Another way your calendar can become a powerful life-guiding tool is by using it to design your ideal week.

Think about what your ideal workweek would look like.

If you're a freelancer, consultant, or coach, it might include focused time to work on client projects, but also time to learn new skills or to be inspired by others' work, or to work on your own marketing initiatives.

If you're a mid-level executive, your ideal week might include one-on-one coaching time with some of your team members, time for a team meeting, as well as time to sit alone to think strategically about the year ahead.

Regardless of your professional role, you may also find that your ideal week—and even ideal day—has some recurring personal things: exercise, time with your family, time to relax or to pursue hobbies.

Mapping all of these items onto your calendar—and making them recurring appointments—is the right way to design your life. It's a powerful way to stay consistent to those activities that give you the most return, and the most joy.

My own calendar reflects many of my values:

- I value health, so I time block 60 minutes each morning for exercise.
- I value coaching my team members, so I time block one-on-one meetings with each direct report on Mondays as a way to kick off the week.
- I value team alignment and breaking down silos, so I time block a weekly full-team meeting.
- I value writing so I have two to three blocks of time scheduled each week to write uninterrupted.
- I value my children's education, so I time block evenings after dinner to help them with their homework.

- I value recharging and new experiences, so I block off long weekends or entire weeks—sometimes a year in advance—for vacations, even if I don't know yet where I'm going.

Remember that the key point is *not* to use a to-do list as your primary time management tool. Items on a to-do list can sit there forever, constantly getting bumped by things that seem urgent in the moment. And having this list of things that still need to get done is the root cause of our underlying stress.

When you master the practice of time blocking—using your calendar instead of your to-do-list—you can literally see your life's priorities by looking at your weekly calendar.

How Does This Apply If You're A(n)...

Entrepreneur: Would it be helpful to block time each week to talk directly to customers, review metrics against goals, or coach your direct reports?

Executive: Would it be helpful to block time for your top objectives?

Freelancer: Would it be helpful to set up time blocks each week to read industry blogs or learn how to use new tools?

Student: Would it help to time block study group time and your teachers' office hours?

Stay-at-Home Parent: Would it be helpful to time block trips to the gym, weekly errands, and bill paying?

SECRET #3

Work from your calendar, not a to-do list.

How much less stress would you feel if you could rip up your to-do list and work from your calendar?

* * FREE BONUS * *

To download the Millionaire Day Planner worksheet and other FREE bonuses, visit:
www.MasterYourMinutes.com

CHAPTER 4

The Procrastination Cure

Imagine if you could use a mental exercise to finally defeat procrastination. How different might your life be?

Procrastination Isn't about Laziness

It's ironic, but I'm procrastinating right now as I write this chapter. I'm supposed to be doing research and customization for a speaking engagement I landed with a giant energy company. But instead I'm writing this chapter. It's not like the motivation isn't there. They're paying me $54,425 to deliver three talks in three days. So I should be jumping up and down for joy and eager to dive in. But alas, writing a book on time and productivity is easier and more fun for me than spending a half day poking around Google Scholar, reading dry academic papers, and creating compelling new slides. Besides, I can get to it tomorrow….

Procrastination is the habit of putting off important, less pleasurable tasks by doing easier, more pleasurable tasks.

Things like email, Twitter, Facebook, food, and TV are excellent ways to procrastinate.

In an interview with the American Psychological Association, Joseph Ferrari, PhD, shared some of his research findings:

> *We all put tasks off, but my research has found that 20 percent of U.S. men and women are chronic procrastinators. They delay at home, work, school, and in relationships. These 20 percent make procrastination their way of life...Let's place the 20 percent in perspective—that's higher than the number of people diagnosed with clinical depression or phobias, two tendencies many people know about.*

To beat procrastination once and for all, you have to understand it. You don't procrastinate because you're lazy. You procrastinate because:

1. You lack enough motivation, and/or
2. You underestimate the power of *present* emotions versus *future* emotions when you set your goals or make your task list.

We tend to procrastinate a wide variety of things. You might procrastinate doing that school report, or making those cold calls, or firing someone who clearly has to go, or cleaning out the garage.

For me, my weak spot is exercise. In every other area of life, once I've decided on the goal, I'm able to execute it without procrastination. But working out? That's a whole other story. So let me use exercise and fitness as our example in the following procrastination busters.

Research Says...

People who rarely procrastinate report higher levels of productivity, happiness, and energy.
(Source: The Kruse Group, 2015)

Procrastination Buster #1: Time Travel

This is a big one. The underlying problem we all have is that we are what psychologists call *time-inconsistent*.

This means we *think* we'll eat salads during the week, so we stock up on lettuce at the grocery store, but inevitably we end up with slimy rotting lettuce two weeks later at the bottom of our refrigerator.

Being time-inconsistent also means we add documentaries and indie films to our Netflix queue because certainly we'll watch them in the future, and yet they never move to #1 because we keep choosing Will Ferrell movies.

And it's why I keep buying new workout equipment and a fancy scale and healthy food cookbooks, and yet I'm still not seeing my six-pack abs.

Despite what we think we are going to want in the future, we have "**present bias**." When the present actually gets here—and yes, the present is always here—we choose candy, sitcoms, Facebook, and cat videos. They're easier and more fun. And hey, we can always get to that other thing in the afternoon, or on Monday, or do the resolution again in January, right?

> **We always underestimate how hard it is to be our best self in the present moment.**

To overcome this time inconsistency, we must do battle with our future self—the one who, in the present moment, will sabotage us. Our future self is the enemy of our best self.

I like to think of this battle as time traveling to defeat my future self. Using the health example, I start by thinking, *how will I sabotage my health goals in the future*? How can I overcome that now?

- My future self is going to sabotage me by eating junk food in the kitchen during my breaks. To beat him, my present self is going to throw out all the junk food and not keep any in the house. I'm also going to buy baby carrots and hummus to reach for as a replacement.

- My future self is going to sabotage my workout by saying it's too busy of a day to fit it in. My present self will defeat him by time blocking exercise first thing in the morning, and I will immediately put workout clothes on as soon as I get out of bed, and I will refuse to look at email until after I work out.

- My future self is also going to sabotage my workouts by thinking *I'm actually pretty healthy, I don't look that bad compared to most people who go to the mall, and my blood pressure and cholesterol are fine*. My present self is going to tell my girlfriend to pinch my love handle flab on any day I don't hit the tread-mill...dang, that will be embarrassing and gross!

One friend of mine goes to extreme measures to battle her five-minute future self! In pursuit of her health goals, when-ever she eats out at a restaurant and they bring her a side of French fries, she immediately opens the salt shaker and dumps the entire thing on top of the fries. She has learned not to trust regular old willpower to not eat the fries. Her five-minutes-in-the-future self is likely to say, "I'll just have one." And we all know how that goes.

How are you going to do battle with your future self?

Procrastination Buster #2: Pain & Pleasure

Ultimately, if we aren't jumping out of bed in the morning excited to tackle our project, it's because our dreams aren't big enough. They aren't motivating enough. And motivation comes down to pain and pleasure. For the tough tasks you always tend to procrastinate, think about and even visualize the "why" behind them.

What pleasure will I get by doing this thing?
What pain will I feel if I don't do it?

One of my enabling goals is to work out every day. Yoga stretches, resistance training, and the treadmill. I need to real-ly pile on the pain and pleasure in my mind to actually do my workouts. *Why do I want to work out? Because I want to look good, I want definition in my abs (come on, what guy doesn't?), I want high energy, and I believe cardiovascular exercise keeps the brain healthy.*

What's the pain I'll feel if I don't work out? I visualize looking flabby with a beer belly (sometimes I don't need to "visualize" it!). I think about that weird pain above my knee that I get when I don't do the pigeon pose in yoga. I think about feeling like a loser, a couch potato, with no energy. I even think about the fact that not working out is disrespectful to my girlfriend.

Does this mental routine sound extreme? I definitely go through this pain and pleasure thought cycle if I'm not feeling motivated, but it's actually helpful to just run through it routinely to burn it into my mindset.

Procrastination Buster #3: Accountability Partner

My childhood friend Curt grew up and became a sports psychologist. He tells me that the number one predictor of whether someone will stick to an exercise routine or not is whether they are doing it with someone else.

This can be a neighbor who meets you every morning at 6 a.m. for a jog. It can be a professional trainer whom you pay $50 an hour to come to your house to kick your butt. It can be your boss who likes to play basketball every day at lunch. It can be a Weight Watchers club where you weigh in every week. And of course, it can be a study buddy at school or just a good friend who is going to check in with you and keep you accountable.

The reason why this is so powerful is that when we procrastinate, we are merely breaking a promise to ourselves; we feel far worse when we break a promise to somebody else.

Procrastination Buster #4: Reward and Punishment

Some people I know respond very well to bribes—even though they are the one in control of the bribe!

One friend told herself she could buy a new pair of expensive shoes, but only after she paid off her credit cards. Another friend bought an excellent bottle of wine but wouldn't drink it until he got down to a certain percentage of body fat.

But in addition to the "carrot," don't forget about the stick approach. Human psychology is such that we actually fear loss more than we want a gain. So instead of rewarding yourself for goal achievement, you can also punish yourself for goal failure.

One company, StickK (http://www.stickk.com/), has made a website that lets you set up a "commitment contract." You pick the goal, the penalty, and a charity of your choice will receive your money if you don't hit the goal. As of this writing, over $14 million has been put up as stakes against goals.

My friend John recently set up a team weight loss goal with his colleagues in the office. Liberal in their political views, they each chipped in $100 and have to donate it to the National Rifle Association if they *don't* shed the agreed upon pounds.

Of course, you don't need fancy software to execute on this strategy. You can always just set up a commitment contract with friends. Give them $100, or whatever amount will "hurt" you, and share your goal. If you don't follow through, they can keep the money or give it to a charity.

Procrastination Buster #5: Act As If...

Be. That's it. *Be*.

Admittedly, this one is a little deep. It has to do with our identity. We all work really hard to stay consistent with who we think we are.

Much of the problem behind task avoidance is that we aren't yet the person we are trying to become. We can visualize our ideal future state, but sometimes the present state—sitting here on the couch watching TV—*feels* a lot better. One unusual but very effective strategy is to self-talk yourself (out loud or in your head) as if you already were your ideal self.

I am a healthy eater. I am a jogger. I am the #1 sales rep in my company. I am a neat person. I am a bestselling author. I am an entrepreneur.

What this self-talk is doing is anchoring your values. If you are already a jogger, it will feel bad and unnatural not to go out jogging today. If you are a writer, of course you are going to sit and write at the computer today—it's what writers do. If you are a healthy person, of course you'll get a to-go salad at the airport instead of a slice of pizza.

Just *be* who you want to become. It will then feel bad—it will be incongruent—*not* to do the task you might be tempted to procrastinate.

Procrastination Buster #6: Settle For Good Enough

Sometimes we find it easy to *start* things, but we procrastinate finishing them. One trick to use is to just plan on settling for less than perfect.

Procrastinating that three mile jog? Well, just suit up and go outside and agree to run around the block once...that will be good enough. And maybe it will be, or maybe once you're done with the block you'll keep going.

Procrastinating finishing that book you've been working on? Well, just agree to push through it sloppily to complete draft one...you can always come back later to revise it.

Procrastinating finishing that new product? Just launch it to the marketplace even if it isn't perfect, and get it closer to perfection each quarter with a new release.

Once you start something, once you agree that imperfect is OK, you'll feel a stronger motivation to finish it up.

How Does This Apply If You're A(n)...

Entrepreneur: Would overcoming procrastination help you to work on the things that feel outside of your comfort zone?

Executive: Would overcoming procrastination make you more effective at having those difficult constructive feedback conversations with your direct reports?

Freelancer: Would overcoming procrastination help you to achieve more billable hours each day?

Student: Would overcoming procrastination help you to complete class projects sooner?

Stay-at-Home Parent: Would overcoming procrastination help you to finally organize the rooms in your house—thus making your mind more peaceful?

SECRET #4

Procrastination can be overcome when you figure out how to beat your future self, who cannot be trusted to do the right thing.

You know what needs to get done this week; how will you ensure that you don't put it off?

** FREE BONUS **

To download your "Procrastination Cure Infographic" and other FREE bonuses, visit:
www.MasterYourMinutes.com

CHAPTER 5

How to Leave the Office at
5:00—Without Guilt

How can the world's most important people always seem so calm, stress free, and fully present in the moment?

Republican political strategist Karl Rove wrote a fascinating op-ed in the *Wall Street Journal*.

> *It all started on New Year's Eve in 2005. President Bush asked what my New Year's resolutions were. I told him that as a regular reader who'd gotten out of the habit, my goal was to read a book a week in 2006. Three days later, we were in the Oval Office when he fixed me in his sights and said, "I'm on my second. Where are you?" Mr. Bush had turned my resolution into a contest.*

> *And the outcome of the bet?*

> *At year's end, I defeated the president, 110 books to 95. My trophy looks suspiciously like those given out at junior bowling finals. The president lamely insisted he'd lost because he'd been busy as leader of the free world.*

The leader of the free world has time to read 95 books in one year?

Sheryl Sandberg Makes It Home for Dinner

Look at the habits of these highly successful business leaders:

- Facebook COO Sheryl Sandberg leaves work at 5:30 p.m. every day so she can have dinner with her kids at 6:00 p.m.
- Former Intel president Andy Grove would arrive at 8:00 a.m. and leave work at 6:00 p.m. consistently.
- Virgin Group founder Richard Branson has over 400 companies in his conglomerate, yet he always seems to be hanging out on his private island or breaking some crazy world record as an adventurer.

Don't you find this shocking? How can they do that?

When I first read about President Bush, I was blown away. You just know the president of the United States of America has a million things to do, right? At the end of the day, there are still more foreign leaders to call and influence, more CIA briefings to read, more campaign contributors to suck up to, more wounded veterans to visit, more voters to rally, more, more, more—and time until the end of his term was ticking away. He had a limited number of days to create his legacy! And yet President Bush "found" time to read 95 books in one year.

Doug Conant, who was the CEO of Campbell's Soup for a decade, used to send out 20 handwritten thank you notes a day. Can you imagine all the responsibilities of being the CEO of a Fortune 500 company? There are always more emails to read, more calls to return, more reports to scan, more meetings to attend, more thinking about the future, and yet...Doug would calmly end his day by hand writing 20 notes.

Back when I was young and dumb, I was running a company that was part of a larger conglomerate. My company was doubling in size every year, and there were never enough hours in the day. I can remember literally jogging through the hallways trying to get back to my office as quickly as possible.

Yet my business partner and boss, Neil, who oversaw my company and 11 other divisions, always moved at a leisurely pace, always had time to tell a funny joke or story, and spent lots of time at the local golf club.

Who has time to play golf? I used to wonder.

The Secret to Guilt-Free Balance

Andy Grove revealed this ultimate secret in his book *High Output Management.*

> *My day ends when I'm tired and ready to go home, not when I'm done. I am never done. Like a housewife's, a manager's work is never done. There is always more to be done, more that should be done, always more than can be done.*

And that is the secret.

> *There will always be more to do, and always more than can be done.*

This is another one of those simple concepts that, once it truly sinks in, can dramatically change your life.

I can remember the very moment I read Grove's book. It hit me like a ton of bricks.

For too long, I let my to-do list master me. "Sorry, I can't make it home for dinner because I still have that report to do."

I never exercised, I skipped most meals, and then I would gorge on fast food. My life was one dimensional, and even in that dimension (business), my around-the-clock pace kept me down in the weeds instead of above the trees.

Super successful people don't just burn hour after hour trying to cross more items off their task list. Instead, they think through their priorities, schedule time for each, and then enough is enough.

George Bush probably valued reading two books a week because it was a way to relieve stress, get smarter, or was just plain fun. He knew that learning and recharging are valuable tasks, and he wasn't going to let them get blocked out by "urgent" items.

Sheryl Sandberg clearly puts a high value on dinner with the family and keeps it scheduled. Yes, she wants to maximize the success of Facebook, but the "success" of her relationship with her children is even more important.

Richard Branson places a high value on fun and adventure and calendars it accordingly. And he smartly crafts his adventures into brand building for Virgin.

Research Says...

People who leave work at a consistent time are less likely to feel "wired" later at night.
(Source: The Kruse Group, 2015)

Do You Need to Be Everything for Everyone?

Jessica Turner, the author of *The Fringe Hours: Making Time for You*, surveyed over 2,000 women for her book and, among other things, asked them to describe the hardest part of being a woman. The common theme: **Being everything to everyone.**

This is something Turner relates to herself. In addition to being a writer, she runs the highly popular Mom Creative (www.themomcreative.com) blog, has a husband, has three children under the age of six, and tries hard to maintain her friendships. She describes how these multiple roles can become unhealthy.

> *For women, this "disease to please" can wreak havoc on every area of our lives. We are nurturers by nature. We want to help and love on others. But sometimes our actions are not an outpouring of love but a result of wanting to please someone else.*

This phenomenon is closely related to the disease of perfectionism. It's dangerous to base our *self*-worth on what *others* think of us.

Many people are surprised that I, a man, can relate a lot to what Turner is describing in her book. Perhaps it's because I'm a single dad and accustomed to maintaining a household.

Regardless of the reason, I still spend too much time—and more importantly, too much stress—on little things that really don't matter.

Recently, my financial advisor told me he was going to be in my neighborhood and wanted to stop by my home and give me an update on my money. It was a sign of high service, and I was grateful.

But my mind immediately took off—*better brew a pot of coffee; is the fridge stocked with Coke? What if he drinks Diet Coke, do I have any of that? We'll be meeting in the kitchen— need to clean the kitchen counter. Is he allergic to cats? I should lock them in the basement...*

It's completely ridiculous to think this way about my advisor making a house call. Among the numerous reasons:

1. He works for me; he'll keep working for me if I keep paying him.
2. He knows far more important things about me—like my net worth—than my kitchen.
3. He's a guy and is probably in awe that another guy is able to keep the house as clean as I do!
4. He knows me personally and I'm sure judges me by my values and kindness, not my hospitality skills.

It is one thing to have good manners and to want to treat friends well and another to *feel like you have to be perfect.* Instead of running around for half an hour preparing for a visitor, I could have just greeted him with a smile and asked, "Can I get you some water?"

As Turner says in her book:

You are never too busy to make time for what you love. It's just a matter of prioritizing—evaluating how you spend your days and dedicating time for what you value. If something is really important to you, you will find a way to fit it into your life.

There Will Always Be More to Do

There will always be more to do in every area:

- You can always do more stuff at work.
- You can always straighten up more rooms and clean more closets.
- You can always do more yard work.
- More, more, more!

So you need to master the practice of letting go of the more, since there will always be more to do.

Once you master this, you'll find it easier to get those workouts in, easier to get home to the family at a reasonable hour, and easier to spend time on yourself without feeling guilty.

How Does This Apply If You're A(n)...

Entrepreneur: Would realizing there will always be more to do enable you to spend more time with your family and friends?

Executive: Would realizing there will always be more to do enable you to hit the gym on a more consistent basis?

Freelancer: Would realizing there will always be more to do enable you to spend more time learning new skills and thinking strategically about your future?

Student: Would realizing there will always be more to do enable you to be satisfied with a good grade instead of a perfect grade?

Stay-at-Home Parent: Would realizing there will always be more to do enable you to give yourself an hour a day—for reading, exercising, or scrapbooking?

SECRET #5

Accept the fact that there will *always* be more to do and more that can be done.

How much better will you feel when you finally accept the fact that you *can't* do it all, because there will always be more that can be done?

* *   FREE BONUS   * *

To download all your FREE bonuses, visit:
www.MasterYourMinutes.com

CHAPTER 6

Richard Branson's Secret Productivity Tool

How can you get your brain to quiet down? How can you always remember your great ideas?

Branson's Most Important Possession

Sir Richard Branson. Arguably the most celebrated entrepreneur of our time. Founder of the Virgin Group, which now comprises over 400 companies, Branson is reportedly worth $4.8 billion.

When asked about items he takes wherever he goes, Branson singled out one item as being most important. In a May 5, 2006, interview he said:

> *It may sound ridiculous, but my most important is to always carry a little notebook in your back pocket. I think the number one thing that I take with me when I'm traveling is the notebook...I could never have built the Virgin Group into the size it is without those few bits of paper.*

Branson, writing on his blog, elaborated on his note-taking habits. He said, "If you have a thought but don't write it down, by the next morning it may be gone forever." One time, when Branson had an idea for a business metaphor, he didn't have a notebook nearby. So he just scribbled the thought down in his passport!

Advice from Billionaire Aristotle Onassis

Greek shipping magnate Aristotle Onassis once gave an interview in which he shared his "million dollar lesson."

> *Always carry a notebook. Write everything down. When you have an idea, write it down. When you meet someone new, write down everything you know about them. That way you will know how much time they are worth. When you hear something interesting, write it down. Writing it down will make you act upon it. If you don't write it down you will forget it. THAT is a million dollar lesson they don't teach you in business school!*

Jim Rohn's Three Treasures

Self-made millionaire and legendary success coach Jim Rohn wrote and spoke frequently about the power of journaling.

> *If you're serious about becoming a wealthy, powerful, sophisticated, healthy, influential, cultured, and unique individual, keep a journal.*
>
> *Keeping a journal is so important. I call it one of the three treasures to leave behind for the next generation...*

The first treasure is your pictures. Take a lot of pictures...

The second treasure is your library. This is the library that taught you, that instructed you, that helped you defend your ideals. It helped you develop a philosophy. It helped you become wealthy, powerful, healthy, sophisticated, and unique...

The third treasure is your journals: the ideas that you picked up, the information that you meticulously gathered. But of the three, journal writing is one of the greatest indications that you're a serious student.

Notebooks of 20 Famous People

The blog *The Art of Manliness* has a great article (http://www.artofmanliness.com/2010/09/13/the-pocket-notebooks-of-20-famous-men/) that shows pictures of the notebooks of 20 famous men including **Mark Twain, George Patton, Thomas Jefferson, Charles Darwin, George Lucas, Ernest Hemingway, Ludwig van Beethoven, Ben Franklin, Thomas Edison, Leonardo da Vinci, Frank Capra,** and **John Rockefeller**.

Although you can see a wide range of notebook styles and penmanship, all show how these great thinkers were never without a means to jot down an observation, an idea, or in Mark Twain's case, dirty jokes.

What Type of Notebook Is the Best?

There are different strokes for different folks:

- Many creative wannabes use Moleskine (http://www.moleskine.com/us/home) notebooks. I use them myself. These high-quality leather-bound books are made in Italy and cost from $9 to $25.
- Some Moleskine fans are switching to Ecosystem (http://www.ecosystemlife.com/) notebooks, including Michael Hyatt (http://michaelhyatt.com/why-i-ditched-my-moleskine-journal.html), because they use recycled paper, are made in the USA, and each page is perforated.
- For many years, I preferred the more expensive and unfortunately very nerdy Boorum & Pease Account Book. It's hard cover, 300 pages so it lasts a long time, thick enough to stand up and stand out on a bookshelf—and so big I never misplaced it.
- Author and entrepreneur James Altucher (http://www.jamesaltucher.com/) recommends waiter's pads, which cost ten cents each. He explains they are the perfect size and a great conversation starter— they also show people you're frugal.

Notice that nobody is recommending yellow legal pads or loose pieces of paper. They are just too easy to get lost in stacks or otherwise damaged. Notebooks are designed to last.

In Their Own Words...

I use this Moleskine notebook that I'll just carry around with me. I make training notes in it. I make work notes in it. I have a whole bookshelf full of old ones at home, because I'll go back and refer to old things in it all the time.

—**Sara Hendershot** *is an Olympic rower for the United States and competed in the 2012 Olympics. She is currently training for Rio 2016.*

I use the Bullet Journal as my go-to organization system. It keeps ideas, thoughts, and other important agenda items at my fingertips. I highly recommend keeping a journal, because a life worth living is a life worth recording.

—**Honorée Corder** *is an author, speaker, and personal transformation expert.*

While apps can be wonderful and help us increase productivity, I prefer to plan in my Moleskine Executive Daily.

—**Natalie MacNeil** *is an Emmy Award-winning media entrepreneur, creator of SheTakesOnTheWorld.com, and author of* The Conquer Kit *(Perigee 2015).*

Take Notes by Hand, Not on a Laptop

Using paper-based bound notebooks for notes is better than taking notes on a laptop, tablet, or smartphone.

Let the hate mail begin!

First, let me say that if you have dyslexia or another learning disability and can really only record notes by typing them into a digital device, *go for it*. It's not a sin, and I'm not trying to bias the world against you.

But if you are using a digital device as a general preference and just think I'm being an old fashioned Luddite, I encourage you to consider an interesting article, "The Pen Is Mightier Than the Keyboard," published in the journal *Psychological Science* in 2014.

Pam Mueller and Daniel Oppenheimer, psychologists at Princeton University and the University of California, Los Angeles, did three different experiments with 327 undergraduates. In one study, students watched a TED talk, took notes, and then took a test on it 30 minutes later. While the laptop users and hand-writers scored the same on factual questions, the laptop users did worse on the conceptual questions.

Noticing that laptop users were transcribing the TED talk instead of noting key concepts, Drs. Mueller and Oppenheimer did a second study and specifically told the laptop users to just take notes in their own words. The results were the same; hand-writers had better recall of the material.

One defense of laptop note-taking is that it enables you to take a more complete set of notes, which is helpful when you need to review the material at a later date. In other words, you'll have more of the raw content to study. So the researchers did a third study in which students took the test a week later, and were given time to study before the test. Once again, hand-writers scored higher.

This latest research from Princeton and UCLA just confirms what others have discovered in the past. The act of taking notes by hand involves active listening, cognitive processing, and finally recalling it to record it. People who take notes with a laptop tend to just robotically record spoken words, without doing the mental work to process it.

And don't forget, if you want to keep a digital, searchable archive of all your notes, you can always scan them into Evernote, use the Jot Script 2 Evernote stylus, or use the Livescribe notebook by Moleskine.

My Personal Notebook System

There are many different fancy Moleskine systems available—including people who cut out tabs or use fancy labeling systems. But you might find inspiration in my Kevin Kruse Moleskine Genius System (OK, I just made that up, I don't have a fancy name for my system). To me, the more complicated I make a paper notebook, the less likely I'll use it. So I just keep it simple.

1. Get yourself a brand new notebook. (I'm back to using Moleskine.) Doesn't it feel great in your hands?

2. Get yourself some Pilot G2 gel pens. They're cheap and a joy to write with. I also like the Sharpie Extra Fine Point pens.

3. Tape your business card to the inside front cover so if you ever leave it behind in a conference room or airplane, a good Samaritan will get it back to you. Some people write, "If found, please call or email me. I will pay a reward to get this back!"

4. Write the current date on the inside cover so you can quickly locate the notebook in the future if you are

trying to find notes from a specific meeting or event. Some people like to use a Sharpie to write the start date on the edge of the pages, so it can be seen without even opening the notebook.

5. Jot down everything and anything you don't want to forget. Record random creative ideas you have: new ideas for books you want to write, companies you want to start, products to invent, new marketing tactics, gift ideas for your family, future vacation destinations, restaurant recommendations, a great bottle of wine, names for your baby, whatever! Write everything down, and you'll never worry or stress out about forgetting something again.

6. Whenever you encounter great advice or an inspirational quote—whether someone says it or you read it—write it down in the back of the book. Reserve pages in the back for these nuggets of wisdom so they can all stay together and be easily reviewed in the future.

7. At the beginning of each phone call or meeting, write the date, time, and names of the people you are speaking with. Jot down any notes from the call, especially any follow-up items or commitments people are making.

8. If you are meeting people for the first time, draw a little diagram of the conference table and write their names in the location where they are sitting to help you remember them. Jot down notes from the meeting but do not try to record everything that is said. You

aren't a court reporter! Just try to record key goals, actions, next steps. Summarize.

9. When you have filled your notebook, write the end date on the inside front cover, again to help you locate the right book in the future when you have a whole row of them on your bookshelf.

10. Put the book up on the shelf next to the previous journals. Here will be a detailed record of your entire life!

11. Every New Year's Day, make it a new tradition to thumb through your old journals from the previous year. You'll be amazed at how much you'll re-learn from your notes, and it will remind you of all your progress. For any thoughts or ideas that you'll want to revisit in the current year, just rewrite them in your new or current notebook.

I also use shorthand that adds clarity to my free-form notes.

- I put an open square (□) next to any item that is a "to do," which I'll put onto my calendar as soon as possible.

- I put an open circle (o) next to any item that is an event to calendar later.

- I put an exclamation mark (!) next to items that require a follow-up action from me.

- I put a question mark (?) next to items that I want to ask about at the end of the meeting.

- I put an asterisk (*) next to items that are important or key themes from an event.

How Does This Apply If You're A(n)...

Entrepreneur: Would a notebook help you keep a record of all the commitments colleagues make during meetings?

Executive: Would a notebook help you record all that you accomplish throughout the year?

Freelancer: Would a notebook help you remember key client obligations?

Student: Would a notebook help you to capture key lecture notes?

Stay-at-Home Parent: Would a notebook help you to capture all the random to-do items that occur each day? Remember, you can review and transfer them to your calendar at a later time.

SECRET #6

Always carry a notebook.

How much less stress will you feel when you begin to dump everything important into your notebook?

** * * FREE BONUS * * **

To download the "Get The Most from Your Notebook" quick reference card and other FREE bonuses, visit:
www.MasterYourMinutes.com

CHAPTER 7

Master Your Email Inbox With 321Zero

How can you empty your email inbox quickly and keep it from interfering with truly productive work?

Email as a Cognitive Slot Machine

According to a survey conducted by the McKinsey Global Institute, office workers spend 2.6 hours per day reading and answering emails, which equates to 33 percent of a 40-hour workweek. (OK, OK, nobody only works 40 hours anymore, but it's *still* a big chunk of an average work week!)

Clearly people send too much email at work, and as the dominant form of professional communication, it's hard to ignore. But you have to take responsibility for your own role in email overwhelm, too.

Your brain uses email—and all social media—like a cognitive slot machine. Like pulling a slot handle, there is anticipation, which feels good as you go to check for new messages. And most of the time it's a bust, nothing there. But every now and then, *ding ding ding, "Oh, look! An interesting article!"* Or even, *"Oh, someone has a question I can answer in only five minutes! I'm so helpful and productive!"*

And our brain releases a bit of dopamine with every triple cherry on the email slot machine. *Ah, that feels good!* Which makes us come back and check it again and again. Yes, you receive too much email, but you need to take responsibility for handling it.

7 Steps to Mastering Your Email

Unsubscribe from email newsletters. Come on! Do you really need to subscribe to all those fashion websites? Those flash deals-of-the-day offers? Those viral clickbait "news" headlines? Don't give permission to all those companies to intrude on your day, to interrupt your flow, to tempt you with their offers. They are trying hard to get into your head, but they can't if they're not in your inbox to begin with! Just go into your email and search for "unsubscribe" and then unsubscribe from all the email newsletters that you find. You can also go to a cool site called www.Unroll.me and it will let you easily unsubscribe from the newsletters you want to trash, and then it will consolidate the newsletters you want to keep into one big daily email.

Turn off all email notifications. Email is not intended to be an urgent form of communication, and especially in these times when most of us are getting 50 to 500 emails a day, getting email notifications is a sin. Notifications interrupt your concentration, your work sprints, and your ability to be present during meetings and conversations. Whether you have an audible ding, a phone vibration, or a little window that pops up with every new email...TURN ALL THAT OFF.

Only process email three times a day, using the 321-Zero system. Schedule <u>three</u> times a day to process your email (morning, noon, night), set the timer on your phone for <u>21</u> minutes, and try to get to inbox <u>zero</u> in that time. Make a game out of it. 21 minutes is intentionally not enough time, but it will keep you focused, ensure that your responses are short, and that you don't start clicking links out onto the wonderful world of internet distractions.

Immediately apply the 4 D's. Every time you open an email, you should be ready to **Do** it, **Delegate** it, **Defer** it, or **Delete** (archive) it.

If you defer an email, in most cases that means immediately adding an entry to your calendar—"moving" the email to a calendar entry (remember, no to-do lists!).

When you think "delete," in most cases you should really just archive. These days, with virtually unlimited storage space, it's easy to just hit the Archive button on most things, knowing that you can use the search function to get it back again in the future.

In addition to the 4 D's, consider F for **File It.** In my opinion, this is just another form of archiving, but it can be helpful especially if you are nervous you might not be able to find something again. Just create folders for all your projects, clients, or even something crazy like "Respond to Someday," and then drag emails related to those topics into the folders to keep your inbox nice and clean.

In Their Own Words...

Meetings, phone calls, and emails can break up your entire day if you let them, leaving you little time to get any big thinking done...Cancel meetings you don't need. And only check email a few times a day.

—Jonah Berger is a marketing professor at the Wharton School at the University of Pennsylvania and author of Contagious: Why Things Catch On.

How do you create an effective work routine? Simple: by choosing what you want it to be, rather than letting others dictate it for you. Except that most people do exactly the opposite, through one simple (terrible) habit: they check their email first thing in the morning...This means that their focus and energy are going where others are directing it, rather than where they stand to make the greatest impact.

—Danny Iny is the founder of marketing education firm Firepole Marketing as well as the bestselling author of Engagement from Scratch! *and* The Audience Revolution.

Think twice before you forward, cc, or bcc. As reported in an August 9, 2013, article in the *Wall Street Journal,* London-based International Power reduced total email traffic by 54 percent just by encouraging their top executives to "think twice" before they forwarded an email or added anyone to the cc: line. Too often we forward or cc someone in the spirit of keeping them "in the loop," but in reality we are contributing to the information overload problem. Remember, every email you send and every cc you include means you are likely going to get a reply back into your own email box. If you *send* less email, you'll also *receive* less email.

Use the subject line to indicate the action required. An ideal subject line doesn't just indicate the subject of the email, but also the type of action it requires. This helps email recipients to process your email in less time. And they'll learn to reciprocate. The idea is to preface your subject line message with some meta-information. I like to use all caps to make this part of the subject stand out from the message. Here are some examples:

- "FYI: [subject]"—Use the FYI designation when you are just passing info along as a courtesy.

- "ACTION REQUIRED by [DATE]: [subject]" or "TO DO by [DATE]"—Use ACTION REQUIRED when your recipients should take an action, but they don't report to you; use TO DO when you are giving a directive to someone who reports to you.

- "NRN: [subject]"—NRN stands for "no response needed" and can be used to eliminate the polite response emails that people often send like "Thanks" or "Looks interesting" or "I'll take a look at this next week," etc.

- "[subject]–EOM"—My personal favorite, EOM stands for "end of message" and lets you put super short messages right in the subject line. EOM tells the recipient, don't bother opening this one because all the content is in the subject line.

Keep emails short—really short. Realize that being brief isn't rude; it's a sign of respect for the other person's time (in addition to your own).

There is even a movement that suggests we consider email messages to be similar to text messages. The website five.sentenc.es suggests you limit all your emails to five sentences or fewer and then add a footer message that directs people to the website for an explanation.

In Their Own Words...

Why use 100 words when 10 words will do. Whether that is in an email, a report, a presentation, or a pitch. Brevity can be powerful.

–Naomi Simson, *founder of RedBalloon, author of* Live What You Love, *and investor on Shark Tank Australia.*

Keep emails short and sweet. Over the years, I've trained myself to write three-sentence emails, leaving out the fluff and keeping only the most essential points. It saves my time and it saves the reader's time.

–Ryan Holmes *is the founder and CEO of HootSuite.*

How to Get to Inbox Zero in Ten Minutes

My friend Christine has over 10,000 emails in her inbox, most of them unread! Perhaps you can relate?

If this is the situation you find yourself in, you might want to declare email bankruptcy and quickly start at "inbox zero" before applying the email management steps in this chapter.

My suggestion is:

1. Deal with all email that arrived within the last 48 hours.
2. Create a folder called Old Emails.

3.   Move ALL of the emails sitting in your inbox into the Old Emails folder.

4.   Voila, you're starting fresh at inbox zero.

Is this sort of cheating? Maybe.

Couldn't you just archive all your emails instead of creating a new folder? Yes.

But why haven't you previously deleted or archived or filed your emails? Why are they sitting there to begin with? Most people tell me that they're afraid there is something valuable that they'll never find again. They don't seem to trust the archive function or know how to use it. So a simple solution is to just create your own labeled folder and move everything there. Enjoy!

How Does This Apply If You're A(n)...

Entrepreneur: Would keeping your email inbox clean reduce your levels of stress and enable you to spend more time on revenue-producing activities?

Executive: Would reducing the time spent on email enable you to spend more time on strategic priorities?

Freelancer: Would reducing the time spent on email enable you to spend more time advancing your skills?

Student: I'm guessing you don't use email very much!

Stay-at-Home Parent: Would eliminating the number of email newsletters you receive help you to spend time more productively?

SECRET #7

Email is a great way for other people to put *their* priorities into *your* life; control your inbox.

Are you ready to commit to checking email no more than three times a day?

* *   FREE BONUS   * *

To download your "Get to Inbox Zero" infographic and other FREE bonuses, visit:
www.MasterYourMinutes.com

CHAPTER 8

Meeting Hacks From Google, Apple, and Virgin

How can you immediately shorten the time spent in meetings by one-third?

Been to a great meeting lately? Yeah, didn't think so. Most meetings are poorly organized, poorly facilitated, and highly inefficient.

In a survey conducted in 2015 by Clarizan, 35 percent of those polled said their weekly status meetings were a waste of time. And if a dozen people are sitting in a one-hour "waste of time" meeting, it's actually a waste of *12 hours*! That's a dozen hours of lost productivity, often to present or review information that could have been covered in minutes through a different medium.

Yet Harvard professor Nancy Koehn estimates that 11 million meetings are held in the U.S. each day!

Why Meetings Suck

Why do the majority of meetings suck so badly?

Meetings start late. Whether a result of unprofessional behavior or the fact that many people literally have meetings stacked back to back, most meetings end up starting late. This becomes a cultural phenomenon as late meetings actually train people to arrive late. When everyone knows the meeting won't start until five or ten minutes past the hour, they don't bother showing up on time. When dozens, hundreds, or even thousands of people in an organization sit around waiting for other people to arrive, those minutes add up to many hours over the course of a year.

The wrong people are in the meeting. The default idea seems to be "When in doubt, invite them!" This wastes the time of the person who was invited (and who may not have the professional courage to say "no thanks"), and if that person feels compelled to ask questions or give input, it wastes the time of everyone else in the meeting, too.

Parkinson's law of triviality. Also known as the bike-shed effect, this law states that organizations spend the most time on trivial issues and the least time on the most important issues. The story goes that a committee must make several decisions related to an expensive nuclear power plant. The approval of the power plant goes quickly with little input because it's too complicated of a topic for most participants to weigh in on. Yet when it comes to deciding on the design of the bike shed for the staff, since everyone understands the trivial project, great time is spent nitpicking and debating it.

Meetings break up the day in illogical ways and may interfere with flow or peak concentration times.

The wrong people dominate meetings. By their nature, the overconfident and the extroverts tend to dominate the communication in a meeting—at the expense of others who may know more but are less inclined to share a meeting format.

The Mark Cuban Meeting Rule

I reached out to hundreds of highly successful people as I was doing research for this book. By design, I was trying to contact the most successful people on the planet, and knowing that they only have 1,440 minutes a day, it never surprised me when people didn't respond to me.

What *did* surprise me was when billionaire entrepreneur Mark Cuban responded to my email only 61 minutes after I sent it.

In his typical direct and to-the-point style, Cuban's time management advice described his approach to meetings.

In Their Own Words...

Never take meetings unless someone is writing a check.

—Mark Cuban *is the owner of the Dallas Mavericks, a serial entrepreneur, and an investor on the TV show Shark Tank.*

Dustin Moskovitz's No Meeting Wednesdays!

If you think Mark Cuban's advice is a bit extreme or impractical, perhaps you can swear off meetings for one day a week.

In an interview for this book, Dustin Moskovitz shared his "NMW" productivity hack, which he brought with him from Facebook.

In Their Own Words...

Pick one day a week that you and your team can focus on getting individual work done without any interruptions like meetings. At Asana, we have No Meeting Wednesdays established to encourage flow and productivity across the company.

*—**Dustin Moskovitz** is the co-founder of team productivity app Asana and co-founder of Facebook.*

Others have taken to this one-day meeting reprieve and called them "Maker Days." The idea is that everyone leaves everyone else alone to focus on "making" stuff—especially if it's making progress on their most important task (MIT).

How to Design Effective Meeting Agendas

If you *have* to have a meeting, highly successful people know that effective meetings begin with effective agendas, which are circulated in advance. Secrets to creating effective agendas include:

- Seek input on the agenda from participants before the meeting, so new topics don't crop up and derail the primary goal.
- Clearly state the purpose of the meeting.
- Clearly state who the facilitator is.
- Identify all invited participants. The fewer the better, but you also want to make sure a key person isn't being forgotten. Google tries to limit meeting participants to ten or fewer. Steve Jobs was known to

throw people out of the room if they couldn't come up with a good reason for being there.

- List agenda topics as questions whenever possible in order to focus the participants on decision-making.
- Attach time estimates to each agenda item so participants can monitor the progress and pace of the meeting; make sure time estimates are realistic.

Google Ventures' Secret Weapon

Jake Knapp, design partner at Google Ventures, is an advocate for using a physical clock to count down the time remaining in a meeting. He discovered a specific type of timer, called the Time Timer, while visiting his child's classroom.

Teachers have been known to call it "The Magic Clock." Coming in various sizes—for about $25 from Amazon.com—the Time Timer is battery powered and large enough to be seen by meeting participants from across a room. A red disc silently spins, showing the amount of time remaining. Why not just set a timer on your smartphone? As Knapp wrote on Medium (https://medium.com/@jakek):

> *The Time Timer is WAY better than a timer app on a screen. Because it's physical, it's easier to adjust and set, and absolutely impossible to ignore.*

During her time at Google, Marissa Mayer was known for using a projector attached to a laptop to display a giant count-down timer up on the wall of the meeting room. I can only assume she still uses this practice at Yahoo!

The Steve Jobs Meeting Method

In 1999, a team of psychologists conducted research on the difference between sit-down and stand-up meetings across 56 different groups. As reported in the *Journal of Applied Psychology*:

> *Sit-down meetings were 34 percent longer than stand-up meetings, but they produced no better decisions than stand-up meetings.*

In a different study, researchers at Washington University in St. Louis determined that standing meetings were far better than sit-down meetings in terms of outcomes. They reported in *Social Psychological & Personality Science* that stand-up meetings led to better collaboration and less possessiveness of ideas, higher levels of engagement, and more problem-solving creativity.

I still remember the first time I sold one of my businesses. Rudy Karsan was the CEO of the acquiring company, and in my very first visit to his corner office, he jumped up before I could sit and said, "Let's go for a walk!" Thirty minutes later, we shook hands on a $2 million deal.

Richard Branson isn't into traditional meetings either. He writes in his blog (http://www.virgin.com/author/richard-branson):

One of my favourite tricks is to conduct most of my meetings standing up. I find it to be a much quicker way of getting down to business, making a decision and sealing the deal. When given the opportunity I often like to take things a step further – literally, with a walking meeting.

Steve Jobs was notorious for his long walking meetings, a practice that has been adopted by Mark Zuckerberg and Jack Dorsey as well.

Marissa Mayer and Richard Branson Hold 10-Minute Meetings

Why do all meetings seem to default to 30 minutes or one hour? It's almost as if people choose that duration because that's the default time block in the Outlook calendar. And we all know that work tends to fill up the space allocated to it.

In an interview with Bloomberg Business in 2006, when Marissa Mayer was still with Google (she now runs Yahoo), she told the interviewer that she holds up to 70 meetings a week. The only way she can cram them all in is to break down the "30-minute" block into small meetings, sometimes as few as five or ten minutes each.

Virgin founder Richard Branson often talks about his aversion to meetings. In a blog post he shared:

It's very rare that a meeting on a single topic should need to last more than 5-10 minutes.

In Their Own Words...

The default length of a meeting or call—both internally and externally—should be 20 minutes; anything longer should be an exception...Even if you're just moving from 30-minute meetings to 20-minute meetings, you can fit in 4-6 more meetings, calls, or appointments in a day.

*—**Ryan Delk** leads growth at Gumroad.*

No Smartphones Allowed

Do you check your phone for text messages or emails during business meetings?

If you answered yes, research from the University of Southern California's Marshall School of Business suggests you are annoying your boss and colleagues. Their study found:

- 86 percent think it's inappropriate to answer phone calls during formal meetings.
- 84 percent think it's inappropriate to write texts or emails during formal meetings.
- 75 percent think it's inappropriate to read texts or emails during formal meetings.
- 66 percent think it's inappropriate to write texts or emails during any meetings.
- At least 22 percent think it's inappropriate to use phones during any meetings.

Why do so many people—especially more successful people—find smartphone use in meetings to be inappropriate? It's because when you access your phone, it shows:

- **Lack of respect**. You consider the information on your phone to be more important than the conversation in the meeting; you view people outside of the meeting to be more important than those sitting in front of you.
- **Lack of attention**. You are unable to stay focused on more than one item at a time; the ability to multitask is a myth.
- **Lack of listening**. You aren't demonstrating the attention and focus that is required of truly active listening.
- **Lack of power**. You are like a modern day Pavlovian dog who responds to the beck and call of others through the buzz of your phone.

To make the most of valuable time spent in meetings, participants should mute and pocket their devices and leave them in their pockets.

Daily Huddles Eliminate Other Meetings

Can more meetings lead to fewer meetings?

I've worked with a lot of consultants over the years, but only Verne Harnish ever gave me the secrets to building highly successful, fast-growing companies. Harnish is the founder of the legendary Entrepreneurs Organization, the CEO of Gazelles and also the author of *Scaling Up*.

One of the big aha moments I had from his work is that an organization can only move as fast as the leadership team. As goes leadership, goes the rest of the company. To make sure everyone is moving fast and staying in sync, it's critical to establish a rhythm or cadence of meetings—the most important being the *daily* huddle.

Initially I was very skeptical.

Daily huddles are quick stand-up meetings with you and your team members. No longer than 15 minutes, always scheduled at the same time each day.

What I quickly discovered is that once daily huddles were in place, they eliminated the need for many other longer one-off meetings, reduced the number of phones calls and emails, and had a dramatic impact on other variables including employee engagement and cross-selling.

The agendas of daily huddles include three things:

- What's up—highlights from the last 24 hours, especially anything relevant to other team members
- Numbers—this is to review any daily metrics, whether sales, conversion rates, or widget production
- Stuck—are you "stuck" on anything, whether it's a problem to solve, red tape to cut, or a question that needs an answer

In Their Own Words...

"Routine sets you free" is the mantra underpinning our tools and approach in Scaling Up companies, including the 15-minute daily huddle with your team (and

spouse!) that will save everyone collectively over an hour each day and allow you to avoid minor train wrecks (that grow into bigger problems) and take advantage of immediate opportunities. "If you want to move faster, pulse faster."

—Verne Harnish *is the CEO of Gazelles.*

Keep your daily huddles to 15 minutes! If they start to run longer, people will be less likely to show up. Force people to be brief, and any "stuck" items that can't be solved immediately should be taken offline.

How Does This Apply If You're A(n)...

Entrepreneur: Would reducing the time spent in meetings enable you to spend more time improving your product?

Executive: Would reducing the time spent in meetings enable you to spend more time coaching your team members?

Freelancer: Would reducing the time spent in meetings enable you to spend more time finding new clients?

Student: Do study groups truly help you with homework, or would you save time studying alone?

Stay-at-Home Parent: How many meetings do you attend in support of the PTA, the soccer league, or other community events? Could you have more impact by actually having fewer meetings?

SECRET #8

Schedule and attend meetings as a last resort, when all other forms of communication won't work.

Look at the meetings on your calendar for the week ahead. How can you eliminate them or reduce their allotted time?

** **FREE BONUS** **

To download your "Maximize Your Meetings" poster and other FREE bonuses, visit:
www.MasterYourMinutes.com

CHAPTER 9

One Little Word That Multiplies Success

Want a one-word magic spell that will instantly free up space on your calendar in the future?

"Focusing is about saying no."—***Steve Jobs***

Email, social media, and text messaging has not only increased the overall amount of information we must deal with, but it has also made it far too easy for other people to ask us for things. Often the requests are social or personal in nature. Want to hang out tonight? Want to go to happy hour? Want to go out to lunch?

And for people who have experienced any amount of business or financial success, the inbound requests to "do lunch" and "grab coffee" flood the inbox each day.

Endless Requests for Our Time

These are the requests I've received in the last 24 hours:

- From a business friend, "Let's grab lunch…"

- From an author acquaintance, "If you have something to say about the book, I'd be delighted if you'd post an Amazon review. You can do it here..."
- From an agent, asking me to include her roster of clients on my "Top 100 Leadership Speakers" list
- From an entrepreneur I've never met, "I am now over here in Boston—a bit of a shock to the system with all the snow— and I'd welcome the opportunity to have a quick five minute call if that was at all possible to say hello and seek your advice."
- From a wonderful, local nonprofit leader letting me know about an upcoming fundraiser, "I hope that everyone on the committee will sell 10 tickets!"
- From the dean of a local college, "I am excited to talk to you about what we are doing here in the business department...Would you be available to meet for coffee one day?"
- Nine emails from readers introducing themselves and telling me about their current challenge.

And then of course are the requests that come through LinkedIn. I get 10–20 messages a day requesting a meeting or call to see if I would like to invest in a company, review a new product offering, provide advice for their startup, help them write their first book, and on and on.

Now don't get me wrong. I'm not complaining about the requests, nor am I making fun of any of the people reaching out. On the contrary, I'm flattered and view these requests on my time to be a sign that I'm doing something right. And in fact, many of these requests I will respond to (coffee with the dean, for example).

But we must be vigilant with our time.

Remember, only 1,440 minutes in a day!

In Their Own Words...

Part of being an Olympic athlete is just that there are a lot of things that I have to miss, and moments or events that I have to skip. I've almost just gotten to the point where I'm used to having to say "No" to things.

*—**Sara Hendershot** is an Olympic rower for the United States and competed in the 2012 Olympics. She is currently training for Rio 2016.*

Even a 30-minute chunk of time for a phone call or coffee meeting means something else won't get done. It could be a poem that never gets written, a chunk of code that doesn't get debugged, a report that doesn't get proofed, a client that doesn't get called back until the next day, two miles that don't get run, or a brilliant idea that never occurs to you. *There is always a price.*

*"The difference between successful people and very successful people is that very successful people say 'no' to almost everything."—**Warren Buffett***

Beware of Distant Elephants

They say that in the distance, even giant elephants at first look small. Unfortunately, many small things turn into big things when they actually arrive.

Research Says...

People who routinely say "no" to requests for their time report higher levels of happiness and energy. (Source: The Kruse Group, 2015)

A young woman, an undergraduate at Dickinson College, emailed me out of the blue one day and told me she was a fan of my leadership work. She said her school had a speaker series each year, and she asked if it was OK for her to suggest me.

Sure, I said. That was my first yes.

A month later, a Dickinson College administrator emailed to follow up with a specific date for me to come speak and to let me know there would be no fee. Would I consider it? My typical speaking fee is $12,500 to $22,500, but I love speaking to students and always try to schedule at least one pro bono speech each month to a nonprofit group.

I looked up the date on my calendar—three months down the road—and that date was free. In fact, my whole week was unscheduled. *Wow, the future was going to really be a lot less busy than the present!* I was looking forward to it. I accepted the invitation. That was my second yes.

As the date got closer, another student asked me if she could interview me for the college radio station. I would have to arrive a couple hours earlier than my event to record the interview. Sure, I said; I'd be honored. That was my third yes.

A week before the event, a professor emailed to ask if I wouldn't mind speaking to his economics class about business and ethics and engagement. His class was earlier in the day. I love speaking to students, I'd be there anyway—just now a little earlier in the day—so, of course, I gave my fourth yes.

As time ticked away and the pro bono event at the college got closer and closer, inevitably things came up. My daughter's school play got scheduled for the same day; I would have to miss it. I was asked to do a corporate keynote event on the same day—for my full fee; I had to turn it down. A TV news program in Australia wanted to do a live interview with me on the same day via satellite, but I was already booked.

Yes, it was a big bummer missing out on all those other things, especially my kid's play, but I don't regret my original decision or the string of yeses that followed.

But I share this story as an extreme example of how *we mistakenly think we'll be less busy in the future than we are in the present.*

It's far too easy to accept a lunch date when you look at your calendar three weeks from now and see that you have no meetings or other lunch plans that day. Sure, that day looks great to grab a casual lunch! And then that day comes, and it's filled with meetings and deadlines and family obligations.

You have to realize: whatever obligations and projects and tasks you have now, you'll also have in a month, six months, or a year. Unless you make a radical change in your life, your kids will continue to get sick, play sports, and require parent-teacher conferences; your boss will still be giving you projects; your car will still need oil changes and inspections; your friends will still be throwing parties.

Every Yes Is a No to Something Else

This is a lesson I even try to teach my kids: every yes is a no to something else. It's not that they should say no to everything; it's that they should think it through.

In Their Own Words...

If something is not a "hell, YEAH!" then it's a "no!"

—James Altucher is a bestselling author, active investor, and host of The James Altucher Show.

Multipliers realize that perfection is achieved not only when nothing more can be added, but when nothing more can be taken away. It is the permission to ignore. Because anything we can say no to today, creates more time tomorrow.

— Rory Vaden is the author of Procrastinate On Purpose *and* Take the Stairs.

True focus is saying no to the things YOU really want to do.

—Nikhil Arora & Alejandro Velez, co-founders of Back to the Roots.

My best tool is to keep front of mind this idea: Everything you say yes to means you are saying no to something else.

—Melanie Benson is the co-author of Entrepreneur.com's Startup Guide to Starting an Information Marketing Business.

My daughter had RSVP'd yes to a friend's birthday party. Then the pop singer Max Schneider announced a local concert date that fell right on the same date. What should she do? Oh the teen angst! She'd told her friend she'd be at the party, and she needed to honor that commitment.

My eleven-year-old son signed up to play travel soccer; he's one of two goalies on the team. After the season was underway, he was asked to play a part in a local play. He really wanted to do it, but the play performance would mean he would miss one or two soccer games. What to do? He made a commitment to his coach and fellow teammates, so he was going to play soccer.

Again, the lesson isn't to *always* say no. Just realize that every yes will be a no to something else when the time comes. Understanding that there is always an opportunity cost will make you hesitate and really be careful about what you are agreeing to put on your calendar.

Why It's Hard to Say No

Despite the fact that "every *yes* is a *no* to something else," we find it so hard to just say no. There are many reasons:

- We're afraid to make people mad.
- We're afraid to hurt someone's feelings.
- We want to be liked.
- We don't want to be rude; we were raised to be polite.
- We underestimate how much time it will really take.
- We aren't clear on our own priorities.
- We feel good by being helpful.
- We like earning future return favors.

Indeed we are raised and socialized to want to help others in need; we value helping others.

But uncontrolled, saying yes to requests for time will quickly block out all the other things we value—including the very things that made us successful in the first place. We are self-imposing the pressure and the feelings of guilt when we say no.

Give yourself permission to say no without guilt. You should not care about what others think of you for declining their requests!

7 Easy Ways to Say No

First of all, know that "no" is enough. You don't owe it to anybody to have to say more than that.

But if you are still struggling with "just say no," then try these more subtle responses. I often send a response email beginning with "Thanks for reaching out..." and continue with one of these messages:

1. "...but I'm on a deadline right now and am not taking any new meetings until I'm done." I use this approach often with strangers who cold-contact me. I don't specify what the deadline is—since they're strangers, they don't need to know my details and shouldn't expect me to share. And the word *deadline* has a magic to it, a power that most people can relate to.

2. "...Unfortunately my schedule is so packed at this time I can only take calls and meetings with paying clients. Thanks for understanding." I use this approach for people who are looking for free advice that

will benefit them and their company tremendously. It's really incredible how often people who already have decent income and assets will ask for time and information that will make them a ton of money, but they don't think to hire someone for the answer. The approach above is a gentle nudge that if they really want to talk to me about their business problem, they can do it if they're willing to pay. They almost always disappear instead.

3. "...and I'm happy to connect, but there is no daylight on my calendar until 2:15 p.m. ET on [*pick a date five months in the future*]." This is what I usually say to someone who I don't know personally but who is vaguely connected in some way. Maybe they are a friend of someone who used to work for me from years ago. The intent of this approach is to not reject them outright, but to let them know I'm hustlin' and have a very busy calendar. This response sends the message that their issue had better be pretty important, and if they really want to meet with you, they'll take the offered time slot in the distant future. I've found that most of these people just respond and say, "Oh, no worries, you sound swamped. Let's just connect when you're less busy." And they go away.

4. "...and my next open slot for a phone call is 2:00 a.m.–2:15 a.m. ET on Thursday of next week. Let me know if that works for you." *Notice the time slot is a.m., not p.m.; that's on purpose.* I only use this line about once a year, because if the person calls my bluff, I'll actually have to stay up late or drag my butt out of bed to take the call. But I use this on people

who are really, really persistent. If I know they're a persistent stranger just trying to sell me something, I can easily say no. But if a friend or business partner suggested they call me, I don't want to ignore them out of courtesy to my friend. But this approach puts a burden back on the requester. How badly do they want to talk to me? Are they really willing to do the call in the middle of the night? Usually they respond with, "Sure, next Thursday afternoon is great, but you had a typo and wrote a.m....that would sure be a crazy time!" I then write back, "No typo. I'm a 24/7 kind of guy, and that's my only open slot for the next several months. Do you want it?" I've never actually had a person in this situation ask for the call, which is really amazing. They are willing to impose on my time to try to get some life- or career-altering information, yet they won't take the call at two in the morning. And, if anyone ever says, "You bet, I'll call you then," I can always respond and say I found a way to move something around and that we can talk during normal business hours.

5. "...but I don't think I'm the best person; I'd like to refer you to..." This is an easy one. People often request your time because they think you know something that can help them or that you are a decision maker that can buy something. If you aren't, or if you've "delegated" that decision making power to someone on your team, use this approach. You can always qualify it by saying something like, "The fastest way to make progress on this is for you to talk directly to my colleague Paulina. But don't worry;

when you're talking to Paulina, you're talking to me. She's the ultimate decider here."

6. "...but I'm not able to take any more meetings or calls during normal business hours. But I often can catch up on emails during travel or at night. Would you like to communicate via email?" This is probably the response I use most often. I really do try to respond to every email I get from readers, email newsletter subscribers, referrals, etc. And email is way more efficient than live phone calls.

7. "...and as a rule, I only schedule 15 minutes for first calls. If you're interested, could you send over a draft agenda so I can see what we'll be covering and what desired outcome you are hoping for?" Again, if you don't want to just reject the person, this type of response is a good way to let them know you're very busy, so if they really want to talk to you, they'd better be willing to do some pre-work. I usually never hear from these people again.

In Their Own Words...

Saying no to friends: Think of the consequences and what the best decision is for you; don't try to please others. Think of yourself first. Be careful of who you surround yourself with; if they're your friend, no will not be an issue.

*—**Haley Silva** is a straight-A student at Sierra High School.*

How Does This Apply If You're A(n)...

Entrepreneur: Would "just saying no" help you to reject tangential meetings from outside parties, enabling you to stay focused on your current product road map?

Executive: Would "just saying no" help you to stay out of nice-to-have initiatives, enabling you to make progress on your quarterly objectives?

Freelancer: Would "just saying no" help to reduce your pro bono hours?

Student: Would "just saying no" help you to spend more time in the library and less time at the coffee shop?

Stay-at-Home Parent: Would "just saying no" help to minimize your "volunteering" and maximize parenting?

SECRET #9

Say no to everything that doesn't support your immediate goals.

Which meetings, calls, and projects will you say no to in the upcoming weeks?

* * FREE BONUS * *

To download your FREE bonuses, visit:
www.MasterYourMinutes.com

CHAPTER 10

The Powerful Pareto Principle

Could a simple analysis of your workload make 80 percent of it disappear?

The Amazing Discovery in an Italian Garden

Vilfredo Federico Damaso Pareto was born in Italy in 1848. He would go on to become an important philosopher and economist. Legend has it that one day he noticed that 20 percent of the pea plants in his garden generated 80 percent of the healthy peapods. This observation caused him to think about uneven distribution. He thought about wealth and discovered that 80 percent of the land in Italy was owned by just 20 percent of the population. He investigated different industries and found that 80 percent of production typically came from just 20 percent of the companies.

> *80 percent of results will come from just 20 percent of the action.*

This "universal truth" about the imbalance of inputs and outputs became known as the Pareto principle, or the 80/20 rule. While it doesn't always come to be an exact 80/20 ratio, this imbalance is often seen in various business cases:

- 20 percent of the sales reps generate 80 percent of total sales.
- 20 percent of customers account for 80 percent of total profits.
- 20 percent of the most reported software bugs cause 80 percent of software crashes.
- 20 percent of patients account for 80 percent of healthcare spending (and 5 percent of patients account for a full 50 percent of all expenditures!)

On a more personal note, you might be able to relate to my unintentional 80/20 habits.

I own at least five amazing suits, but 80 percent of the time or more I grab my black, well-tailored, single-breasted Armani with a powder blue shirt. (Ladies, how many shoes do you own, and how often do you grab the same 20 percent?)

I have 15 rooms in my house, but I spend about 80 percent of my time in just my bedroom, family room, and office.

I'm not sure how many miles of roads are in the small town where I live, but I bet I only drive on 20 percent or less of them.

On my Samsung S5 smartphone, I have 48 different mobile apps pinned to the tiles, but 80 percent of the time I'm sure I'm only using about 8 of them.

When I go grocery shopping, I definitely spend the most time in the aisles that are around the edges of the store: produce, the fish market, dairy, breads—and generally skip the aisles in the middle of the store (except health and beauty).

As a massive introvert, I don't actually socialize too much, but you probably find that you spend 80 percent of your time with 20 percent of your friends and family members.

In Their Own Words...

I accept that I cannot do everything so I work only on things that are vitally important using the 80:20 rule.

> **–James Schramko** *is the founder of SuperFastBusiness.*

The two primary productivity concepts I apply are the following...First, the 80/20 rule, which helps me to identify which tasks deliver the biggest rewards and thus I should focus on. Two, the "Theory of Constraints," which helps me to identify what the immediate constraint is that's holding me back from a desirable result.

> **–Yaro Starak** *is the author of the blog* Profits Blueprint *and founder of the Entrepreneurs-Journey.com blog.*

So how can we apply Pareto's principle to gain more time in our lives?

80/20 Business

In business, you could literally analyze your customer base and decide to "fire" 80 percent of the least profitable customers. I certainly fired many clients who weren't worth the trouble back in my day.

You could do the same with your sales force. Apply the 80/20 rule and fire the majority of your sales representatives who are actually producing the least. This will enable you to reward the remaining highly successful reps with more accounts or larger territories and give you more time to support the "winners" on your sales team.

You could look at all the products you are currently offering and, using 80/20 analysis, get rid of the majority of your products that provide the least profit. This could eliminate the majority of customer service issues, free up room in your warehouse, and simplify your value proposition.

If you're running a software company, make sure you are identifying which bugs are causing 80 percent of the phone calls to your help center. Eliminate these first, and you'll dramatically reduce your tech support costs.

You can even apply 80/20 to your marketing efforts. I once interviewed Seth Godin at a conference and asked him why he didn't use Twitter. This was back when Twitter was all the rage and, given that Seth is viewed as a marketing guru, people were shocked he wasn't engaged with the platform. He said, "I have nothing against Twitter. There are only so many hours a day and if I spend time on Twitter, I won't be spending time on other things, like writing a daily blog post."

In this age of social media, so many of us feel like we have to be on Twitter and Facebook and LinkedIn—my gosh, I even have a Pinterest page! But a simple 80/20 analysis would reveal that most of your engagement, most of your audience, probably comes from just one platform. You could let people know that's where you'll be, and then ignore the rest.

80/20 Yardwork

How much time and money do you spend on your yard each year? Maybe your current practice is to mow the lawn, edge the lawn, apply fertilizer or other chemicals, weed the flower beds, trim the bushes and trees, plant flowers, and sweep the sidewalk. If you don't do it yourself, think how much you spend on mowing, replacing mulch, buying lawn fertilizer, applying weed killer, or trimming trees.

The 80/20 rule would suggest that only 20 percent of yard maintenance activities account for about 80 percent of how your yard actually looks to the neighbors and others who are driving by your home. With that in mind, you might decide to mow and weed, but stop edging and planting seasonal flowers. (Unless yardwork is fun for you, of course!)

80/20 Reading and Studying

My favorite high school teacher gave me sound advice as I went off to college. She warned that the reading assignments would be unlike anything I had done before. A book a week for classes using fiction, and multiple chapters a week from each textbook.

She taught me that if you just read the first and last paragraph of each chapter as well as the first sentence of each paragraph in between, you'll understand 80 percent of the message of the book. I learned that it might not get you straight A's, but it can get you solid B's.

Today, I have three over-scheduled kids in school. As I help my teenage daughters study for high school tests, I now know to start by looking at the chapter summaries and chapter self-tests. Knowing what the textbook author thinks is most important, and then going back and finding the answers to those questions in the text itself, is much more efficient than reading the entire chapter from beginning to end.

What's in the Dalai Lama's Bag?

My favorite story about the Dalai Lama was from an article in *The Globe and Mail* in 2002. The Dalai Lama travels the world frequently, teaching people about Buddhism and the plight of the Tibetan people. A man without many possessions, he always carries a small red bag wherever he goes. According to the reporter at one event, someone in the audience asked the Dalai Lama what was in his bag.

Immediately, he opened it and began pulling out objects for all to see. A chocolate bar, a case for his glasses, a toothbrush, Kleenex tissues, and then after a pause—a single candy, which he promptly unwrapped and popped into his mouth.

How much stuff do you carry with you when *you* travel? Is too much "stuff" taking away your time?

Most of my friends have second homes. Some are in New York, others at the Jersey shore, others have ski cabins in the Poconos. They are surprised that I don't have a vacation home. What they don't realize is that I've listened very carefully when they talk about their homes. Rarely do they talk about how much joy they are getting from them. But I definitely hear it when they tell me that they have to deal with the aftermath of a break-in, or that Hurricane Sandy put three feet of water in their first floor, or that they've rented it out and someone trashed the place.

A second home is just one example to show the truth that all objects come with a cost, like collectible knickknacks that need to be dusted every week. The bigger the house, the more rooms that need to be cleaned. Electronic gadgets need to be learned, set up, stored, Bluetooth-paired, and ultimately fixed! Pools need to be cleaned. Pets need to get walked, groomed, and taken to the vet. Boats put in and taken out of the water.

With three school-age kids, I think my suburban lifestyle is practical. But once the kids are all out of the house, I will be too! I envision getting rid of almost everything I own (I'll pack up the sentimental stuff—there won't be much—and put it in a climate-controlled storage facility) and just spend a year renting an amazing apartment in a different city each year until I get bored with that or die. New York, Barcelona, Amalfi, Sydney or Melbourne, Hong Kong, La Jolla or Napa, who knows where!

The lesson isn't that all "things" are bad—I have some toys to drive and two cats. It's just that all things require time, and we should think twice before acquiring them.

While we may not want to limit our possessions to only that which fits into one small red bag, we can probably take inspiration from the Dalai Lama, who clearly doesn't need objects to feel happy.

The 80/20 Mindset

The important takeaway from this chapter on the Pareto principle is not to run around with a calculator and actually do the math to figure out 80 percent and 20 percent calculations in different areas of your life.

It's more important to have a mindset of identifying the few things and activities that will give you outsized returns. You want to:

- Look for shortcuts.
- Do the most important things exceptionally well, and the rest just "good enough" or not at all.
- Develop your skills to be exceptional in a few targeted areas; don't try to master everything.
- Realize that you can work less, stress less, and increase your happiness by figuring out the 20 percent of goals and activities that are most important to you.

How Does This Apply If You're A(n)...

Entrepreneur: Would an 80/20 mindset help you to stay focused on your strategic plan and spend less time chasing endless new opportunities?

Executive: Would an 80/20 mindset help you to maximize the return from your limited resources?

Freelancer: Would an 80/20 mindset help you to focus on and service your most important clients?

Student: Would an 80/20 mindset help you to identify the content that matters most on a test?

Stay-at-Home Parent: Would an 80/20 mindset help you to manage the household without losing your mind?

SECRET #10

Eighty percent of outcomes are generated by twenty percent of activities.

What 20 percent of your time generates 80 percent of your value?

---

* * FREE BONUS * *

To download your FREE bonuses, visit:
www.MasterYourMinutes.com

CHAPTER 11

The "3 Harvard Questions" That Save 8 Hours a Week

Can three simple questions save you eight hours a week?

The Slacker Who Won a "Best Coder" Award

In January of 2013, several news outlets reported on the remarkable story of Bob.

With Bob's programming speed and code quality, his company named him "Best Coder in the Building" and gave him an excellent performance review. He was a model employee; in his mid-40s, Bob clocked in by nine each morning and sent his boss a daily summary of his productivity before he left at five.

But if we had been able to secretly peek over Bob's shoulder all day—to discover how he spent his time—we would have seen something peculiar. On Bob's typical day, he would read Reddit and watch YouTube videos from about 9:00 to 11:30, which is when he would head out to his 90-minute lunch. Back at 1:00 p.m., Bob would then spend the next three and a half hours on Ebay, Facebook, LinkedIn, and other social media sites. At 4:30, he would send a report to his boss and go home—without writing a single line of code. The next day would be the same.

How could this be? How could "Bob" be his company's star programmer, yet goof off all day?

It turns out that Bob was very smart.

Instead of asking, "How can I do this?"

He asked, "How can this get done?"

The answer, in Bob's case, was that he outsourced his task—actually his job—to a software development company in Shenyang, China. Bob's company gave him approximately $200,000 a year to do his work, and he in turn gave $50,000 a year to a programmer in China to do it for him.

For the longest time, Bob's company marveled at his productivity and quality, while he surfed the Internet eight hours a day.

Eventually Bob's company noticed unusual server access from China, and thinking they were being hacked, they stumbled on Bob's brilliant scheme. They were not amused. Bob was fired.

Research Says...

People who actively look for things to delegate report higher levels of productivity, happiness and energy, and are less likely to feel "overworked and overwhelmed." (Source: The Kruse Group, 2015)

If *I* had been the CEO, I would have doubled Bob's salary and made him the CTO. That way he could have outsourced all the development work and saved the company millions of dollars.

While Bob ultimately got fired for breaking company rules, we can learn a lot from his approach to getting things done.

In Their Own Words...

See your day from a higher perspective...Avoid leveraging your time for money, instead leverage your expertise and delegate the rest.

—Jeff Moore is president of two seafood companies and the founder of a global mastermind group called Thursday Night Boardroom.

Drop, Delegate, or Redesign

In September 2013, Professors Julian Birkinshaw and Jordan Cohen shared the results of their productivity experiment in the *Harvard Business Review*.

They found that 41 percent of knowledge workers' time is spent on discretionary activities that weren't personally satisfying and could also be done by others.

So why do people keep doing these activities?

The researchers suggest that often we feel important when we feel busy; we feel engaged and satisfied as we make progress against tasks, and while meetings are often boring, they also provide an opportunity to leave the desk and socialize a little bit.

Once workers were trained by Birkinshaw and Cohen to *slow down* and think about their activities in a new way, they achieved massive time gains.

In fact, on average, *the workers who were trained saved six hours of desk work and two hours of meeting time each week.*

So what's the secret to these massive time savings?

The researchers trained everyone to analyze their tasks to see if they could:

- **Drop**: What items can I drop? What can I stop doing entirely?
- **Delegate**: What items can I delegate to a subordinate? What can I outsource?
- **Redesign**: What do I need to continue doing, but do it in a new, time-efficient way?

To put this into practice, make a list of all the tasks and meetings you worked on during the previous week and follow these steps:

1. Ask, "**How valuable is this task to me or to the company**? What would happen if I just dropped it completely?"

2. Ask, "**Am I the only person who could do this task**? Who else in or outside the company could accomplish this?"

3. Ask, "**How can the same outcome be achieved but with a faster process**? How could this task get completed if I only had half the time?"

Those three questions will give you the data you need to identify the tasks that are of low value and should be targeted to Drop, Delegate, Redesign.

In Their Own Words...

Leverage every dime you have to outsource and buy other people's time. That is the key. Organize your 168 hours, then BUY hours from others to grow.

—Shane & Jocelyn Sams *built a high six-figure business selling digital products and started FlippedLifestyle.com to help other families "flip their lives" with online businesses.*

Tony Robbins Was a Teen When He Hired an Assistant

I can remember being 25 years old and mowing my lawn on a hot Saturday in August. I was the CEO of a startup, working over 80 hours per week, barely getting any sleep, getting no exercise, and I had no social life, and yet there I was spending a couple hours mowing and edging my lawn.

Sweat dripping off my chin, face baking in the sun, straining up the grassy hill, pushing the mower through a cloud of dirt and grass pollen, all the time thinking about the slide deck I needed to create before Monday, the hundreds of emails I needed to respond to, not to mention painting a bedroom, doing the laundry, and going grocery shopping.

So why didn't I just hire some kid to mow my lawn for me? Because I had no money. I should say I *thought* I had no money.

I recently watched an interview with Tony Robbins. He tells a similar story of starting out—still just a teenager—and realizing that as broke as he was, he was going to hire help, initially for just two hours a day. He tells his story:

I think in the very beginning the hard thing is you think you can only do it yourself and then there's only so many hours and you've got kids and family and friends and how do I do it all?

The answer is you hire someone. You trade with someone. You trade them for 2 hours. That's what I did in the beginning. Because I remember, I remember, I'll never forget, I was just really young in my career, very in the early days, and I was running to get to the dry cleaners so I could get my only two suits because if I didn't get them, you know, then the place closes and I can't get on the plane.

And I was running to the airport sweating like crazy, and I'm a sweater anyway. Sweating like this, trying to get in the door, and it was like, what is wrong with this picture?

I could be doing something that's so productive and I'm standing in line at the dry cleaning place. This is just nuts. And so I was really... I was like 17, 18, 19, I don't know what I was, and I said, "I'm gonna hire somebody." Two hours a day, that's what I need to start with. And then it was 4 hours.

And so my view is I don't do anything that someone else can do better, and I don't do anything that isn't the highest and best use of my time.

You need to start paying other people to do stuff for you even before you feel you are ready. What would it cost to hire the kid down the street to mow your lawn each week?

Are you a stay-at-home dad? What would it cost to hire an unemployed college grad to watch your kids for an hour each afternoon to let you have some alone time?

In Their Own Words...

Nothing will slow you down, take you off track, or keep you unproductive more than doing things which you both: do not like to do and are not good at. Anything that falls into that category must be outsourced to someone else (ideally who both likes it and has competence) as soon as possible. The extent to which you continue on those types of tasks is what will hold you back from truly loving what you're doing and also being fulfilled.

*—**Andrea Waltz** is the co-author of the bestselling book,*
Go for No!, *and a professional speaker.*

I outsource anything I can using fantastic tools like Amazon Prime for two-day shipping and Peapod for grocery delivery so I don't have to go to the store; FancyHands.com to book appointments, look up vendors, research products, etc.; Thumbtack for finding any household task that can be done; and ZocDoc for making doctor appointments. Being a mom of two little ones and running a multi-office agency requires all of the help I can get!

*—**Kim Walsh-Phillips** is a leading direct response social media marketer, bestselling author, keynote speaker, and founder of IO Creative Group.*

Venture Capitalist Suster on the Value of an Admin

Are you a startup CEO? What would it cost to hire a really good administrative assistant? Why spend money on an admin when you know how to use a computer and can do it yourself?

There are only two blogs that I read religiously, and venture capitalist Mark Suster writes one of them. In *Bothsides of the Table* (http://www.bothsidesofthetable.com/), Suster gives advice to startup entrepreneurs. In his article "The Controversial First Role to Hire After Your 'A Round,'" Suster makes a compelling case for the value of an admin.

> *Your first hire after that first round of capital is an office manager/company-wide assistant.*
>
> *"What? You're joking, right?"*
>
> *No.*
>
> *While I'm passionate about being scrappy when you start and controlling your costs, I'm equally passionate about performance when you have a bit of cash. And I've seen way too many CEOs/founders get bogged down in minutiae because they were used to it from the scrappy phase. They've struggled to scale.*
>
> *Think about it. Your single most valuable asset in the early days is your senior team and presumably nobody is more valuable than the founding team. And you're bogged down in expense claims, booking hotel rooms, scheduling meetings, dealing with a leaky toilet, processing payroll, ordering computers, etc.*

If you don't *have* an admin, you *are* an admin.

Even if you can do all the administrative work yourself, why should you? The one hour a day you spend running to the post office, balancing the checkbook, or booking airline tickets would be better spent calling prospects, learning, or thinking strategically. Always try to spend as much time as possible using your unique strengths on your highest leverage activities. Running out to Staples to buy printer paper probably doesn't fall into that category.

In Their Own Words...

Focus on what you are great at and hire everyone else to do the rest.

—Lewis Howes *is a bestselling author, entrepreneur, and former professional athlete. He is the host of* The School of Greatness *podcast.*

Today You Can "Uber" Everything

Ever since the success of *The 4-Hour Workweek* by Tim Ferriss, using virtual assistants has been somewhat in vogue. Initially, using a virtual assistant, or VA, generally meant working with someone in India or the Philippines to screen your email, schedule appointments, and other general tasks. While some found these arrangements to be helpful, others found the language barriers and the lower quality of work to be unacceptable.

But since the early days of VAs, the concept has really grown and morphed into the idea that you can outsource almost anything, with very little prior planning.

Uber was really the company that popularized the concept of on-demand mobile service (ODMS). Remember being envious of the "rich and famous" with their chauffeurs? Well in the same time it would take you to say, "Home, James," you can now tap your Uber app and have your personal chauffeur show up to take you to your destination.

Spend too much time grocery shopping? See if Instacart (www.instacart.com), Peapod (www.peapod.com), or Fresh Direct (www.freshdirect.com) operates in your area. For non-perishables, use Amazon.com Subscribe & Save (www.amazon.com/gp/subscribe-and-save/details/).

Need someone to do some Internet research, make social media updates, make reservations at a restaurant, or cancel your cable? Just visit FancyHands.com.

Have miscellaneous chores to complete? See if the folks on TaskRabbit (www.TaskRabbit.com) will hop over to clean your oven, build your Ikea furniture, or organize your closets.

And don't forget, for all your general freelance needs: www.fiverr.com, www.freelance.com, and www.upwork.com.

When *The 4-Hour Workweek* first came out, outsourcing was a novelty. Now, it's just assumed you can give the work to the best people, and nobody cares where they are located. With WiFi Internet access, Skype, email, and project management communication tools like Asana (www.asana.com) and Slack (www.slack.com), working with remote team members has become no big deal.

I live outside of Philadelphia and personally use "virtual" help for all kinds of things:

- Clarissa is one of my book cover designers; she lives in Singapore, and I have no idea what she looks like (we've only communicated via email).
- Balaji lives in India, and I've used his team to do research projects, data mining, and slide designs.
- Serena answers my Mailchimp email technical questions (when we first connected, she was spending time in Ireland, and now she's in Thailand).
- Camille is one of my book editors whom I found on www.Fiverr.com (her profile page says she lives in the United States, but I have no idea where).
- Matt and Chris are the two guys who handle my websites (I've never had a face-to-face project meeting with them).

In addition to the team of remote freelancers I routinely work with, locally I also outsource these items:

- I pay $60 a week to a company to mow my lawn.
- I pay $100 to a guy to plow my driveway when it snows.
- I pay $150 every two weeks to a cleaning service to clean my house.
- I pay $20 an hour to a woman to help me get my kids off to school each morning.
- I pay a bookkeeper to handle both my personal and business accounting needs; I never write a check myself.
- I hire plumbers, electricians, and painters to maintain my home.

But Mark Cuban Still Does His Own Laundry

So what shouldn't you outsource?

Notice that while I have someone who stops in a few mornings each week to help, I've never had a full-time nanny for my three kids. While I have good friends who have live-in nannies or daily full-time nannies, I just never felt comfortable with that myself. For me, I don't want a non-family member living in my house, and parenting is my first value, so I want to do it myself as much as I can. I'm fortunate in that I have a lot of schedule flexibility that enables this. *I'm not judging others who are making different choices*; I do it consciously, knowing that it is costing me potential income and career advancement.

I also do my own grocery shopping—almost every day or every other day actually. This makes *no sense* from a time optimization standpoint. But I actually like it. I like having the freshest fruits and vegetables and fish possible, and zipping quickly through the store is my way of going to the market each day. Since I work from home, it's a good excuse to get some fresh air and sunlight.

Billionaire Mark Cuban revealed on *Shark Tank* that he still washes his own laundry. I do, too. It would be easy for me to have someone stop in each week to do my laundry or to drop it at the dry cleaning place—it would be easy for you to do that too, and maybe you should. But I just find it grounding somehow to do my own laundry.

The bottom line is you should try to outsource everything you can unless:

1. You enjoy doing it and it's part of your rest and recharging process.
2. It's part of your values to continue doing the task.
3. It costs you more per hour to outsource it than you want to make yourself.

In Their Own Words...

Every year, audit your time and find a way to delegate at least 15% of what you're doing.

—Jay Baer *is the founder of Convince & Convert, a keynote speaker, and author of* Youtility.

How Does This Apply If You're A(n)...

Entrepreneur: Would being aggressive about outsourcing help you to spend more time using your unique abilities?

Executive: Would being aggressive about outsourcing enable you to reduce project costs?

Freelancer: Would being aggressive about outsourcing enable you to spend more time utilizing your true talents?

Student: Would being aggressive about outsourcing (your laundry perhaps?) help you to spend more time studying for the big exams?

Stay-at-Home Parent: Would being aggressive about outsourcing give you a few hours to exercise or recharge?

SECRET #11

Focus your time only on things that utilize your
unique strengths and passions.

What are you going to outsource starting next week?

* * FREE BONUS * *

To download your FREE bonuses, visit:
www.MasterYourMinutes.com

CHAPTER 12

Why Twitter Co-Founder Jack Dorsey Themes His Days

What if one simple change to your calendar enabled you to have a quantum leap in your productivity?

Jack Dorsey's Productivity Secret

Jack Dorsey is the co-founder of Twitter and the founder and CEO of Square. For a while, Dorsey worked full time at both companies. Sixteen hours a day—eight hours at each. In a 2011 interview at Techonomy, Dorsey explained his secret to his productivity.

The only way to do this is to be very disciplined and very practiced. The way I found that works for me is I theme my days. On Monday, at both companies, I focus on management and running the company...we have our directional meeting at Square, we have our OpCom meeting at Twitter, I do all my management one-on-ones on that day. Tuesday is focused on product. Wednesday is focused on marketing and communications and growth. Thursday is focused on developers and partnerships. Friday is focused on the company and the culture and recruiting. Saturday I take off, I hike. Sunday is reflection, feedback, strategy, and getting ready for the week.

And there are interruptions all the time, but I can quickly deal with an interruption and know that it's Tuesday and I have product meetings, and I need to focus on product stuff. It also sets a good cadence for the rest of the company. We're always delivering; we're always showing where we were last week and where we're going to be the following week.

How John Lee Dumas Themes His Days

John Lee Dumas built a million-dollar business in a few short years on the success of his daily podcast, *EntrepreneurOnFire*. Dumas' colleague, Kate Erickson, wrote a 2014 year in review blog post in which she described the impact daily themes have had on their business.

Something that we also both found success with doing is creating themes for each day of the week. For example, John's podcast day is Tuesday: that's when he does all of his podcast interviews for EntrepreneurOnFire.

Another example: Wednesdays are our webinar days. This is when we schedule our Live Podcast Workshops, our Webinar Workshops, and our exclusive community webinars.

Having themes for our days makes it easier to plan ahead, and easier to stay on track. Having an entire day set aside for a theme creates a bigger space in which to accomplish things, and a smaller chance that you'll "just set it aside" until tomorrow.

Three Themes from Dan Sullivan

Renowned entrepreneur coach Dan Sullivan suggests that we theme every week around three different kinds of days:

Focus Days: "Game days" are to focus on our most important activities, typically revenue-producing activities. These are also the days when we should ideally be using our unique talents; do what you do best.

Buffer Days: These are days to catch up on emails and calls, hold internal meetings, delegate tasks, catch up on paperwork, and complete any training or educational activities that are related to work.

Free Days: These are days without any kind of work. These are days for vacation, fun, or perhaps charity. No work-related emails, calls, or thinking should be done on these days; it's a time to rejuvenate.

Designing My Ideal Week

I try to theme my days as well, but not quite to the point of Dorsey, Dumas, or Sullivan. Here's what my typical week looks like:

Monday: The first day of the week is my day for internal management meetings (similar to Dorsey). I meet one on one with each direct report as a way to review key developments from the previous week and to review activities and goals for the week ahead. I also end the day with a team meeting where everybody briefly shares what their week looks like so there is a contextual awareness within the company. To be honest, I don't like Mondays because I don't like meetings. But I love starting each week with a "huddle" that I know will make the next four days highly productive.

Tuesday through Thursday: The days in the middle of each week are my "focus" days. In my current business, these are the days that I spend writing new books, designing e-learning courses, or writing marketing material. Those items are the "output" that generate revenue and are definitely utilizing my unique strengths.

Friday: The end of my week is my "buffer" day that I use to process bills, catch up on email, or respond to readers.

An Office Hour Theme

In addition to my days-of-the-week themes, I also theme the last Friday of each month as my day to book lunch or coffee appointments.

I'm inundated with "can we grab a coffee" requests each week, and for those invitations I want to accept, I just give them the next open time slot on my last Friday of the month. The waiters at LaStalla in Newtown are always amused as I arrive at 11:00 a.m. and just sit at the same table as a string of guests come and go each hour. I pick up the bill at the end of the day, which usually includes three or four lunches (I only eat one) and about ten coffees.

Bestselling author Dave Kerpen similarly "themes" a block of time on a weekly basis for outside meetings. He explained to me, "While I take meetings with just about anyone who wants to meet with me, I reserve just one hour a week for these 'office hours.'"

Sandwich Vacation with Buffer Days

I used to hate vacations. They stressed me out.

The idea of vacation was fine, but then the day before vacation would be an insane scramble of trying to hand things off while doing a normal day's work. The first few days of vacation would consist of me either dealing with the undone things via phone and email or worrying about those things if I was trying to "unplug." The day back from vacation would make me nauseous, scrambling again to catch up on emails and calls while diving back into a normal day of meetings.

To gain a quantum leap in vacation quality, just schedule a buffer day before and after your vacation. Bookend your vacation with days that are time blocked for catching up. No pre-planned meetings, no project work, no lunch catch-ups. Just block out that time—especially the day back from vacation—to catch up on emails, phone calls, mail, and quick stand-up meetings with staff to get back up to speed.

Just knowing you have this time to hand off work in an organized fashion, and then time to catch up again, will help you to truly rest and relax while you're away.

Want the secret to making this work? Tell your admin which day you'll be returning to work, but tell him or her to leave "vacation" marked on your calendar for everyone else to see. That way you won't get scheduled into meetings or have people pounce on you as soon as you walk in the door.

How Does This Apply If You're A(n)...

Entrepreneur: Would it be helpful to theme product development and customer acquisition days?

Executive: Would it be helpful to time block internal meeting times, but also free thinking times?

Freelancer: Would it be helpful to theme one day a week just to deal with pesky things like finding clients and sending invoices?

Student: Would it help to theme one night a week as "party night" and another night for "study in the library time"?

Stay-at-Home Parent: Would it be helpful to theme Sunday afternoon as time to pre-cook a week's worth of meals?

SECRET #12

Batch your work with recurring themes for
different days of the week.

How much more productive would you be, how much less stress would you feel, if your days were organized to maximize your effectiveness?

---

* * FREE BONUS * *

To download your FREE bonuses, visit:
www.MasterYourMinutes.com

CHAPTER 13

Don't Touch!
(Until You're Ready)

Can one small change in your habits gain you dozens of minutes each day and free up mental energy?

How Do You Sort Your Mail?

You can tell a lot about people by how they go through their daily mail. Here's how I used to do it…

After a long day at work, I come home, grab the mail from the box and walk back into my kitchen. Curious and procrastinating, I flip through the stack. Junk mail, electric bill, junk, mortgage statement, junk, junk, magazine, hand written card with no return address, junk, junk, car loan, junk, junk.

The small card certainly stands out, and I open it right away. It's an invitation for my son to go to a birthday party in a few weeks. I pull up the calendar on my iPhone. It looks like he'd be able to go. I'll have to double check there are no other plans.

I put the card down and open the electric bill. I've been blasting the air conditioning so much I wonder how big the bill is. Yikes! I decide to open the other bills to glance at when they're due.

I set the bills down and pick up BusinessWeek and flip through the pages, reading a couple headlines and thinking I'll have to remember to come back and read one of the articles.

Finally, I put the magazine down on the island and begin to cook dinner. Later that night, I'll return to the mail, sort through it, and throw out all the junk mail. I'll leave the magazine in the kitchen (cluttering my environment) and toss the rest on my desk in the office. In the days ahead, I'll reopen the bills to pay them and, if I remember, reopen the invitation, glance at the calendar again, and send back an RSVP.

While this type of "processing" of mail might not seem like a big deal, it's often a sign of how we do everything: we come back to things *over and over again*.

When we process our email, we might respond to each "ding" by scanning who it's from and what the subject line is. We then decide whether or not to open it. If we open it and read it, we then decide to leave it in our inbox so we can respond to it later...when we'll read it all over again.

We might take off our dirty clothes and throw them on the floor in our bedroom. Later we pick them up and throw them in a pile in the closet. Once a week—or when we can't actually close the door to the closet any longer—we get a laundry basket and put the clothes in it and then take it to the washing machine. Later we'll come back and actually start a load of laundry.

'Touch It Once' Mentality

Highly successful people take immediate action on almost every item they encounter. They know that to be efficient, they want to expend the least possible amount of time and mental energy processing things. In short, they practice a "touch it once" mentality.

Here's how I now go through snail mail using the "touch it once" principle:

- I walk out to the mailbox and grab the mail.
- As I walk back up my driveway, I pick out all the junk mail.
- I toss the junk mail into the recycle bin in my garage before I even walk back into the house.
- I easily pick out the magazines and put them in my magazines-to-be-read stack on the coffee table.
- I take the remaining bills—that's all there is left, nobody sends letters anymore—and set them on my bills-to-be-paid pile next to my computer.
- Because I've time blocked 30 minutes every Friday morning for paying bills, I don't even bother opening those envelopes until that time.

I actually think the 'touch it once' rule is so important I recommend you immediately take action on something if it will take *five minutes or less* to complete. As long as it won't interfere with a pre-scheduled task, you are generally better off taking immediate action than having to come back to it in the future.

In Their Own Words...

Whenever I have a small task that needs to be completed (that takes less than five minutes), I should complete it now, rather than putting it off. This ensures that I do not have a long list of tasks that I have to complete later at the end of the day.

*—**Nihar Suthar** is a straight-A student at Cornell University.*

'Touch It Once' for Email

Most people read each email item as soon as it appears, or they open their inbox, see a bunch of new messages, and immediately click each message to open it and read it.

Unless a reply requires only a couple of words, most people close the email message to deal with later—when they'll have to open it and read it all over again!

The better way is to process every email message immediately. Here's how I actually actioned my email this morning, along with the internal debate that occurred in my mind.

11:00 a.m. My morning health rituals are complete, my kids are off to school, and I've finished two hours of focused writing time. Time to open my email accounts...deep breath.

The first email is a Google alert that I've set up to monitor my own name. It shows that my previously scheduled blog post went live this morning. I hop over to my blog to make sure it's all good and notice a typo right in the title of the blog post. Damn, I'll have to fix that in a few minutes after I scan the rest of my emails.

No! Touch it once, my inner voice reminds me. I quickly open WordPress, fix the typo, and click Publish.

The next email is from a freelancer giving me his employer identification number (EIN) so my accountant can prepare a tax document. I'll have to send that along with a note to my accountant later.

No! Touch it once. I hit Forward, add a few lines, and off it goes to my accountant.

Next email is from my lawyer, and an invoice is attached. *What?! I wasn't expecting a bill.* Double-click the PDF. Yep, it's correct, I had forgotten about his work on my trademark question. *Ugh, I just finished paying bills yesterday.*

I can print the invoice and place it in my bills-to-be-paid pile for processing during my normal weekly bill-paying time block, or touch it once. *Do it now!* Fortunately my lawyer takes credit cards. I fill out the credit card information on his website and send it back—it took only three minutes.

Next email...I recently joined the Pennsylvania Society and sent them my dues. Somebody needs to know if it's a nonprofit or not. *How the heck do I know? Who can I pass this on to? Oh sheesh, let's just deal with it right now.* I open a new tab in my browser and go to their web page. Quickly scan their About page. No mention of 501(c)3 nonprofit status. Reply to email: Don't think so. Send. Done.

Next email...Someone asking about my speaking fee and availability. I forward it to my virtual admin. Don't even type anything in it; she'll know what to do.

After I either clear out all the emails or come to the end of my 30-minute time block, I just close my email completely and come back to it again late in the afternoon.

'Touch It Once' and Calendar It

A *very* powerful tactic is if you can't take immediate action on an email, just calendar it for future action. Remember, we want to use a calendar, not a to-do list.

For example, my sister Debbie just sent me an email. Instead of replying to it, I'd like to call her to have a more detailed live conversation. But I don't add it as a task at the bottom of a to-do list. And I don't leave it in my email inbox, where it might get buried or never actioned. Instead, I set up a time on my calendar to "Call Sister Debbie."

I use Gmail and Google Calendar, so when an email message is open and I want to create a calendar appointment for it, I just:

1.   Click the "More" button (drop-down menu) near the top center of the window.
2.   Choose the "Create event" option from the drop-down menu.
3.   A new tab opens up displaying a new event form in Google calendar; it defaults to the current day and time and puts the email subject line as the event title. The body of the email appears in the Description field.
4.   Adjust the date and time as desired and click "Save." Voila!

If you're using Microsoft Outlook as your email client, it's even easier. While your email is open, just click the "Schedule" button, or you can even drag an email onto a calendar date on the right side of the screen.

For more information or to find screenshots of how to do this, just Google "how to create a calendar entry from email."

'Touch It Once' to Declutter

A messy environment can be mentally taxing, increase the time it takes to find stuff, and eventually demand scheduled time to "clean the house." A touch-it-once mentality can go a long way to keeping your environment tidy all the time.

I'm teaching my three kids to practice 'touch it once.' They used to take their dirty dishes and put them on the counter near the sink. I would eventually have to go to the sink again, pick them up again, and then place them in the dishwasher.

Now they know when they're done with their meal to pick up their plate and glass, rinse them in the sink, and put them directly in the dishwasher.

Same with their laundry. No more taking their shoes or socks off and throwing them on the side of the couch to be forgotten. If they take their shoes off, they immediately take them to their room or put them by the door.

When it comes to laundry, I even put two laundry baskets in my walk-in closet. One is for dark colored clothes (cold water) and the other is for whites (hot water). Why pick up and sort all the dirty clothes when the sorting can be done when I throw it in the closet?

How Does This Apply If You're A(n)...

If you're an **entrepreneur** or **executive**, would "touch it once" help you to keep on top of your email inbox?

Freelancer: Would "touch it once" help to keep your administrative paperwork in order?

Student: Would "touch it once" help you to power through each subject's assignment?

Stay-at-Home Parent: Would "touch it once" help to keep the house clean and all that paperwork your child's school sends home completed?

SECRET #13

If a task can be completed in less than five minutes, do it immediately.

How much time will you gain when you aren't returning over and over again to "touch" the same items? Touch it once, touch it once, touch it once.

* * FREE BONUS * *

To download your FREE bonuses, visit:
www.MasterYourMinutes.com

CHAPTER 14

Change Your Morning, Change Your Life

Imagine if you could have a solid hour of daily "me time" that could drive higher levels of happiness, productivity, and creativity throughout the day.

It is far too easy for us to wake up, feel the pressure of our never-ending to-do list, and immediately begin to react. React to overnight email messages, react to social media, and react to the first item on our calendar.

Even if we had intended on having a healthy breakfast at home or jumping on the treadmill, when we go into reaction-mode it's easy to think, *I'll grab coffee on the road and work out tonight—better get into the office and get some of this stuff done.*

Highly successful people design an empowering and energizing morning routine and stick with it.

In Their Own Words...

I wake up fully rested, spend 30 minutes in meditation *and then go to my workout area. While working out physically, I take advantage of the rich audio programs available so that I fill that 45 minutes with physical exertion combined with mental input and expansion. I never check the news or look at my iPhone first thing in the morning, no matter how important it may seem to know the latest news…I carefully protect that first hour of the day, making sure that all input is positive, clean, pure, creative and inspirational. Many of my most creative ideas have come from this protected time of the day, often when I am in a full sweat. By 9:00 AM I am invigorated, motivated and ready to face anything the day may bring.*

> *—Dan Miller is the author of the New York Times best-selling* 48 Days to the Work You Love, No More Dreaded Mondays, *and* Wisdom Meets Passion.

Get up 15 minutes earlier than everyone else in your house and get into the office 15 minutes before everyone else. You can solve any problem in your life if you devote 15 minutes of focused thinking to it first thing in the morning every day.

> *—Craig Ballantyne is the creator of Turbulence Training and is the editor of EarlyToRise.com.*

My "Sacred 60" Morning Routine

In the introduction of this book, I shared a story from a time when I was young and dumb, overworked and out of control, and would leap from my bed to the shower to my car in under 20 minutes. That was when I sped right past a state trooper without realizing he was there, until he pulled me over.

Looking back, I can see that not only was I living dangerously, but that lifestyle was impairing my creativity, ability to think strategically, and overall productivity.

Well, no more buttered rolls and flying past cop cars for me! These days my mornings look something like this:

6:00–6:20 a.m.—Get up, feed the cats, turn on coffee pot, prep kids' lunch or breakfast items while drinking coffee, hug kids out the door to school.

6:20–6:21 a.m.—Guzzle protein shake and water.

6:21–6:22 a.m.—A minute of gratitude.

6:22–6:27 a.m.—Concentrative meditation.

6:27–6:40 a.m.—Turn on podcast, do yoga stretches.

6:40–6:50 a.m.—Resistance training: one muscle group.

6:50–7:00 a.m.—Shower, dress.

7:00 a.m.—Begin work on MIT without interruptions.

I consider this to be a very minimal "hour of power." During less busy times, I add 30–60 minutes of cardio while listening to an audio book or podcast.

It's pretty amazing how different I feel since I've started this practice:

- I feel better as a parent knowing that I got a touch point of love with my kids.
- I feel full but not sluggish with the protein breakfast, and the water seems to wake me up.
- My "attitude of gratitude" increases and extends my happiness.

- I personally don't notice any benefits from meditation, but I believe the scientific research behind it, and I'd probably get more from it if my practice were longer than five minutes.
- The simple yoga stretches have been a life changer; pushing 50 years old, I immediately feel pains and tightness throughout my body if I forget to stretch.
- Listening to audio books or podcasts while stretching or doing cardio means no matter what else happens later in the day, I feel good knowing I already had some "me" time for learning or entertainment.

The Morning Routines of Arnold Schwarzenegger, Tony Robbins, and Other Highly Successful People

Obviously, successful people don't all follow the exact same routine, but it is amazing how you can easily identify consistent themes.

- Most wake up early—6 a.m. or earlier.
- They hydrate by drinking *a lot* of water.
- They eat a healthy breakfast, although each has a different definition of healthy (e.g., fruit and oatmeal, green smoothie, protein, slow carb).
- They exercise.
- Many meditate, journal, or read.

In a video spot recorded for Tim Ferriss, **Arnold Schwarzenegger** shared his daily morning routine:

My morning routine is very simple. I get up every morning at 5:00 in the morning, and then I go downstairs to the kitchen, start reading the various different newspapers, and then go on my iPad, do all my e-mails and stuff like that...go upstairs to the gym and work out 45 minutes to an hour, do cardiovascular training...Then after that, have my breakfast. Usually, it's oatmeal, bananas and strawberries and some blueberries in there, I mix it all up, with some coffee, eat that, go take my shower, and then go to work.

In his audio program *The Ultimate Edge*, **Tony Robbins** shares his "hour of power." He begins each morning with a series of breathing exercises, followed by ten minutes of contemplating everything he is grateful for and visualization of everything he wants in his life. He then spends 15–30 minutes doing some kind of exercise while repeating incantations. In a recent interview with Tim Ferriss, Robbins shared that he now practices cryotherapy each morning, too, standing in a chamber that drops to around -166 F° for a couple minutes.

Shawn Stevenson is a health and fitness expert, bestselling author, and host of the podcast *The Model Health Show*. In an interview for this book, Shawn shared his morning routine:

Energy is everything. We have a certain amount of willpower allotted to us every day, and we burn through it quickly if our energy is low. I like to do most of my creative work in the morning, so I make sure that I stack the conditions in my life to ensure that my energy is high when I get to my laptop. There are three things that are mandatory for me when I wake up.

First, I take what I call an "Inner Bath" by drinking about 30 ounces of high quality water. This helps to jumpstart your metabolism by flushing out metabolic waste products accumulated in your body while you were asleep. Whether you realize this consciously or not, when you wake up you are dehydrated. This will help to instantly balance your body out.

Second, I do a short session of exercise—20 minutes or less—like rebounding (using a mini-trampoline), going for a brisk walk, or doing Tabata (which only takes four minutes!) This is not done for the purpose of getting 6-pack abs (although it couldn't hurt), it's done for the purpose of releasing endorphins that make you feel good and stress hormones like cortisol and epinephrine that help you to focus (and research shows that secreting these hormones in the morning will actually help you to sleep better at night).

Third, I eat a lower carbohydrate, higher fat, moderate protein breakfast.

Business Insider ran a series where they asked highly successful people to reveal their morning routines.

- **Gary Vaynerchuk**, co-founder and CEO of Vayner-Media, gets up at 6 a.m., does a news and social media scan, and then works out with a trainer for 45 minutes. He calls family members on his drive into the office.
- Cartoonist **Scott Adams** practices the same morning routine every day, including weekends and holidays. He wakes up at 5 a.m., but he told Business Insider, "...if I wake up any time after 3:30 a.m., I call that close enough and pop out of bed with a hum and a bounce." His morning meal is coffee and a protein bar.

- Entrepreneur and Shark Tank investor **Kevin O'Leary** wakes up at 5:45 a.m. and watches the news while riding an exercise bike for 45 minutes.

- FOCUS Brands president, **Kat Cole**, wakes at 5 a.m. and drinks 24 ounces of water while checking social media for about 20 minutes. She does 20 minutes of exercise and eats a high-protein snack.

- Author and professor **Cal Newport** rises at 6 a.m., drinks a glass of water, and then walks with his dog. While in the park, Newport stops and bangs out 25 pull-ups.

Hal Elrod's 6-Step Morning Routine

Hal Elrod (www.halelrod.com) is a professional speaker, success coach, and author who credits his morning routine with turning his life around and establishing a solid foundation for his success. In fact, he believes so strongly in the power of morning rituals, he even wrote a book about it, called *The Miracle Morning*. In an interview, Elrod told me:

> *The premise of* The Miracle Morning *is to wake up and start each day with the discipline of dedicating time to personal development, so that you can become the person you need to be to create the most extraordinary life you can imagine, and do so faster than you may currently believe is possible. While most people focus on "doing" more to achieve more,* The Miracle Morning *is about focusing on "becoming" more so that you can start doing less, to achieve more.*

Through Elrod's research and own experiences, he developed a system he calls *Life S.A.V.E.R.S.*

- S is for Silence (quiet, gratitude, meditation, or prayer)
- A is for Affirmations (purpose, goals, priorities)
- V is for Visualization (of goals or ideal life)
- E is for Exercise
- R is for Reading (a self-improvement book)
- S is for Scribing (journaling)

Elrod makes a compelling case that no matter what level of success you already have, using your first minutes of each morning to invest in yourself will take you to an even higher level.

How Does This Apply If You're A(n)...

Entrepreneur: Would starting your morning with a "sacred 60" routine facilitate ideation and keep you grounded through the inevitable challenges of running a startup?

Executive: Would starting your morning with a "sacred 60" routine give you the physical and mental health to have a successful career over the long haul?

Freelancer: Would starting your morning with a "sacred 60" routine increase your hourly productivity throughout the day?

Student: Would starting your morning with a "sacred 60" routine help you to reduce stress during exam weeks?

Stay-at-Home Parent: Would starting your morning with a "sacred 60" routine increase your patience and happiness?

In Their Own Words...

The morning ritual that has become sacred to me is a 35-minute power walk first thing. Getting outside, breathing the fresh air, clearing my mind and resetting my focus all results in a powerful start to an amazing day.

—*John Lee Dumas* is the founder and host of EntrepreneurOnFire, which generates over $250,000 a month in revenue. Dumas offers a free 15-day course on podcasting at FreePodcastCourse.com.

Power mornings: make everything you do for the first 120 minutes a ritual, including 30 minutes for light exercise, stretching and meditation.

—*Jeff Moore* is president of two seafood companies and the founder of a global mastermind group called Thursday Night Boardroom.

My best productivity tip is to wake up early. An early start to the day provides time for introspection and preparation. I generally try to get into the office by 6:30am.

—*Chris Myers* is the co-founder and CEO of BodeTree and a frequent contributor to the Wall Street Journal, Forbes, Entrepreneur Magazine, *and* MSNBC.

SECRET #14

Invest the first 60 minutes of each day in rituals that strengthen your mind, body, and spirit.

What time will you set your alarm clock, *for tomorrow morning*, **so you'll have time for your morning ritual?**

* * FREE BONUS * *

To download your "Change Your Morning, Change Your Life Worksheet" and other FREE bonuses, visit: www.MasterYourMinutes.com

CHAPTER 15

Energy Is Everything

Would you like the *real* secret to completing twelve hours of work in just an eight-hour day?

You Can't Get More Time, Only More Energy

What if the ultimate time management secret isn't about time at all? You can't "manage" time—no matter what you do, you will have the same 24 hours tomorrow that you had today. When people talk about "time management," what they really want is to get more stuff done with less stress. And the real secret behind this is that you need to maximize your energy.

I saved this secret for the end because I didn't think you'd even read it or care about it if I put it up front. But it's the most important secret of all.

Red Bull Nation

Have you ever been reading a book, but you keep reading the same paragraph over and over, and it's still not sinking in?

Have you ever been working on an important report, and you keep zoning off into space—wasting how many minutes doing nothing?

Do you get sleepy an hour or two after lunch? How productive are you then?

Have you ever actually fallen asleep at your desk? How about right in the middle of a meeting?

Have you ever been in a brainstorming session, but you just couldn't come up with any good ideas?

If you said yes to most of those questions, you can personally understand that our physical and mental energy varies— and that it has a direct effect on our productivity.

In Their Own Words...

Don't sacrifice your sleep. Sooner or later, it will catch up with you. You won't perform at your best, and you will get sick.

*—**Will Dean**, an Olympic rower for Canada, competed in the London 2012 games. He is currently training for Rio 2016.*

Did you know that consumers buy over four billion cans of Red Bull each year? The company behind 5-Hour Energy power shots reportedly makes more than $600 million in revenue annually.

People everywhere are fatigued and looking for a quick fix. But while an energy drink might bring short-term alertness, it's no way to handle the chronic brain fatigue so many of us have come to view as normal.

How Monica Leonelle 6x'd Her Productivity

I am a writer.

I write slowly. This is a problem. Because…I am a writer.

About a year ago I tracked my productivity and learned that I write on average 500 words per hour. Most professional writers produce at least twice that amount.

So in order to make better progress on my next book—this book actually—my natural inclination was to "time manage" my writing. I could make a list of all the things I needed to write. I could prioritize them and make sure I was spending time writing this book each day. I minimized distractions and said no more often. I tried to "find" more hours in each day, each week, and each month. I even outsourced some research, like the time management quotes you'll find at the end of this book.

And all of that helped to a degree.

But then I noticed that writing came easily around eight in the morning. Kids off to school, I'm feeling fresh, and my coffee is kicking in. I checked, and my average words per hour in the morning was about 750–1,000. But then I checked my productivity in the afternoon—getting a little tired and already thinking about the nightly activities—I discovered that my word count was about 250 per hour. Yes, my overall average was 500 words, but the same chunk of time, 60 minutes, produced dramatically different results *based on how I felt* in the moment.

In Their Own Words...

I have to know when I'm at my best for my most important work (morning, for writing fiction), when I tend to slack off (after meetings or podcasts), and when I can get by with relatively mindless work (afternoons). It's not about getting maximal amounts done; it's about ideally matching my capacities vs. my occasional need to screw around with what needs to be done at what time.

–**Johnny B. Truant** *is a co-host of the top-rated* Self-Publishing Podcast, *co-author of* Write. Publish. Repeat: The No-Luck-Required Guide to Self-Publishing Success, *and the author of well over 2.5 million words of popular fiction.*

In *Write Better Faster*, author Monica Leonelle shares how she went from being a 600-word-per-hour writer to a 3,500-word-per-hour writer. She learned that:

- When she repeated cycles of a 25-minute writing sprint followed by a 5-minute break, she achieved a 50 percent improvement in productivity. With these short recharging breaks, Leonelle was able to maintain a near state of flow for longer periods of time throughout the day.

- Her ailing wrists and fingers caused her to rethink her tools. She switched from keyboard typing to dictation and gained an additional 33 percent in word count.

- Once freed from the keyboard, Leonelle gained a final 25 percent improvement in word count when she began to dictate her novels while walking outside.

Leonelle didn't have more hours to give, so she figured out how to increase her *energy* instead, and her productivity gains were the same as if she had "found" six times more hours!

In Their Own Words...

It is important to schedule time for yourself, to rest, or to refocus.

> —*Katie Uhlaender is an Olympic skeleton racer for the United States and competed in the Olympics in 2006, 2010, and 2014.*

Get your blood pumping for at least a minute or two every day. Quick workouts give a huge boost to energy and feed the brain with the oxygen you need to take over the world.

> —*Abel James is a bestselling author, musician, and host of the #1-rated health podcast* Fat-Burning Man.

Don't sacrifice sleep for productivity. Many young entrepreneurs believe they can function on little sleep while they build their business. But lack of sleep (and, more importantly, lack of brain rewiring from adequate rest) can cause you to lose your edge and sharpness.

> —*Mark Sisson is the author of the best-selling book* The Primal Blueprint *and owner of Primal Nutrition, Inc.*

The Most Productive People Take More Breaks

Tony Schwartz, founder of The Energy Project, teaches that human beings are designed to "pulse" between expending energy and renewing energy. His research shows that humans naturally move from full focus and energy to physiological fatigue every 90 minutes. Our body sends us signals to rest and renew, but we override them with coffee, energy drinks, and sugar or just by tapping our own reserves until they're depleted.

Schwartz suggests that we need to purposely take short breaks every 90 minutes throughout the day to drink water, walk, or to eat healthy snacks. His mantra is, "Pulse and pause."

The idea of pulsing energy is behind the increasingly popular Pomodoro Technique developed by Francesco Cirillo (and used by Leonelle, as mentioned earlier in this chapter).

With the Pomodoro method, you set a timer for 25 minutes, work on a single task with your full focus, then take a 5-minute break to get up, move around, maybe drink some water. Then repeat the cycle.

The Draugiem Group installed software that tracked the time and productivity of all their employees. They discovered that their top ten percent most productive employees didn't actually work any more hours than anybody else. In fact, they took more breaks. On average, this high-productivity group worked for 52 minutes and then took a 17-minute long break.

In the examples above, we see recommendations to sprint for 25 minutes, 52 minutes, or 90 minutes, all followed by breaks. The important point isn't the exact length of the sprint or the break, it's to figure out what "pulse and pause" cycle works best for you. Our cognitive capacity declines throughout the day; you must build in frequent mental breaks to recharge and maintain productivity.

In Their Own Words...

Work in short bursts of productive work, instead of long, unproductive sessions (in which 80% of the time is spent on Facebook). Strategies like the Pomodoro Technique...reduce distractions and increase productivity.

*—**John Ramos** is a straight-A student at the University of Coimbra in Portugal and is a writer at TheStudentPower.com.*

Set a timer for everything you do. When you have a deadline you are more productive. I use the Pomodoro technique...

*—**Ian Cleary** is founder of Razorsocial, an award-winning marketing technology blog.*

I believe that I can get any task completed (even hated ones) in 25 minutes...open tomato-timer.com (it's a free website), hit start on a tomato, and then dive into whatever task I find myself procrastinating on.

*—**Christie Mims** is the founder of the Forbes Top 100 Website for Careers, The Revolutionary Club.*

Energy Starts with Health

The biggest way to increase your overall energy levels is of course to take care of your health. You already know this, but keys to productivity include:

- Getting enough sleep
- Minimizing alcohol

- Minimizing caffeine, especially late in the day
- Eating more whole foods and fewer processed foods
- Maintaining a healthy weight
- Drinking a lot of water
- Exercising daily (a 20-minute power walk counts!)

In Their Own Words...

For me, it's a daily workout during my lunch hour that keeps me sane. On most days, by 1:00 p.m. I have already put in about seven hours of work. At that time, it's a no-brainer that I need to recharge and refresh so that I can handle the second half of my day with the same focus and energy as I did the first half.

*–**Mohammed Dewji** is the CEO of Tanzania-based MeTL Group. Forbes has named Dewji the youngest billionaire in Africa.*

Make intense exercise a daily habit. The more fit I feel, the clearer my head is, the better decisions I make, and the more success I seem to attract.

*–**J.T. O'Donnell** is the CEO of CareerHMO & Careerealism. Her work has been cited in the* Wall Street Journal, USA Today, New York Times, The Boston Globe, *and others.*

How Does This Apply If You're A(n)...

Entrepreneur: Could increasing energy and alertness (enabling you to achieve more in the same amount of time) help you to get more balance in your life?

Executive: Would increasing energy and alertness (enabling you to do more in the same amount of time) help you to get home for dinner with your family?

Freelancer: Would increasing energy and alertness help you to be more productive during sleepy afternoons?

Student: Would increasing energy and alertness (enabling you to do more in the same amount of time) reduce the number of your all-night cramming sessions?

Stay-at-Home Parent: Would increasing energy and alertness give you more patience with family members?

SECRET #15

Productivity is about energy and focus, not time.

How will you increase your energy tomorrow?

* * FREE BONUS * *

To download your FREE bonuses, visit:
www.MasterYourMinutes.com

CHAPTER 16

The E-3C System: Putting It All Together

How can you condense the 15 secrets of time and productivity into an easy-to-implement system?

In Their Own Words...

I stay productive by developing and maintaining what I call a personal "operating system," which is a set of processes, tools and checkpoints that define how I get work done every day. The specifics of an operating system differ from person to person, but the important thing is that you have one.

*—**Corbett Barr** is co-founder and CEO of Fizzle, a community and training platform for entrepreneurs.*

Remember, there is no one system that universally works for everyone; you don't need to incorporate all 15 secrets to see improvements in productivity. The most important thing is to learn from the habits shared by highly successful people and adopt them in a way that works for you and your situation.

In order to help you to take immediate action, I've simplified the findings from all of the research into a simple system that I call **E-3C**. **The E stands for Energy, and the three C's are Capture, Calendar, and Concentrate**.

Energy

The first step—the most important part of my E-3C system—is "E" for Energy.

You can't make more time, but you *can* increase your productivity. Increasing your energy and focus is the most important secret to achieving 10x productivity in the same amount of time.

Highly successful people get enough sleep.

Highly successful people eat energizing foods and exercise consistently.

Highly successful people maintain morning rituals—like meditating, journaling, hydrating, practicing yoga—that establish a foundation of energy, clarity, and alertness for the entire day.

Highly successful people pulse and pause throughout the day to maintain peak performance.

Capture

The first "C" in my E-3C system stands for Capture.

You must "capture" everything and anything into a notebook instead of trying to keep things in your head. In a best-case scenario, trying to remember to-dos, to-calls, and to-buys leads to a higher cognitive load and unnecessary stress—worse, it can lead to incomplete tasks.

Highly successful people keep a **notebook** with them at all times and write down everything they want to remember. In addition to capturing to-do items, they also record notes from calls and meetings, new ideas, lessons learned, favorite quotes, and other things that might need to be referenced in the future.

Think of your notebook as your external brain. The more you put into it, the less filled your biological brain will be!

I believe paper-based notebooks (like Moleskine or similar designs) work best; you can always scan your written notes into Evernote later—or even better, have your admin or virtual assistant do it for you!

Additionally, this practice improves your effectiveness, as you no longer forget important things to do, can hold other people accountable, and can learn from your accumulated written experiences.

If you are writing things down that you need "to do," remember: as quickly as possible, you will want to schedule it as an appointment on your...

Calendar

The second "C" in my E-3C system stands for **Calendar**.

What is implied with this step is ***don't use a to-do list***! If you want "to do" something, immediately schedule it on your calendar.

Highly successful people have clearly identified values which lead to top priorities and their Most Important Task (MIT). You must time block MIT time on your calendar. Time for other activities that support your top values (e.g., health, relationships, giving back) should also get blocked on your calendar on a recurring basis.

Highly successful people theme days on their calendar, too. At work, Monday might be the day for one-on-one meetings or for a weekly team huddle. Wednesday might be themed as "no meetings" or "afternoon office hours." At home, Sundays might be the day for grocery shopping, laundry, and cooking a full week's worth of healthy meals in advance.

Highly successful people protect their calendar, knowing and feeling the reality that nothing is more important than time. They say no to anything and everyone who does not align with their priorities and are especially wary of "distant elephants." They do something only if they aren't able to drop it, delegate it, or redesign it. They spend time on the 20 percent of things that contribute 80 percent of the value—and they drop the rest.

Concentrate

The third "C" in my 3C system stands for Concentrate.

Highly successful people proactively work from their calendar; they don't react to stimuli like incoming email, social media messages, or "got a minute" meetings.

Highly successful people don't multitask; they concentrate on one task at a time.

Highly successful people concentrate on their MIT and other priorities during times of peak energy, typically in the morning.

Highly successful people pulse and pause to maintain concentration and productivity throughout the day. Most take 5-minute breaks every 30 to 60 minutes.

In Their Own Words...

Do one thing at once. Stop multitasking!

—Mike Cannon-Brookes is the co-founder of Atlassian, an Australian software company.

The basic principle of time management is as follows: do one thing, and one thing only until it is finished, then move on. This means put your phone away so texting, Snapchat, Twitter, and Instagram aren't distracting you while doing homework.

—Elizabeth Poblete is a straight-A student who attends Xavier College Preparatory.

Your mobile device? Turn off ALL notifications. Only look when you have time or when you have scheduled time to deal with it. Granted, I have a unique tone for my wife, but that's about it. Don't let technology control you... you control your technology.

—Mitch Joel is president of Mirum, a global digital marketing agency. He is the author of Six Pixels of Separation *and* CTRL ALT Delete.

The Time Is Always Now

I don't collect art. But when I accidentally stumbled on a mixed-media painting by artist Peter Tunney, I had to buy it at any cost. Its simple message: the time is always now.

Be mindful.

Live with intention.

Remember, there are only 1,440 minutes in a day.

CHAPTER 17

20 More Time & Productivity Hacks

The 15 secrets shared above are the principles that are most likely to get you massive gains in productivity. Below are even more tips and tricks you can use to save time.

1. **Always cook more than one meal at a time.** There is a lot of inefficient time in cooking. The planning, shopping, prep work, cooking, cleaning. If I cook dinner, which is often, since I enjoy cooking, I'll make sure I get two or three different meals out of it. I personally don't mind eating the same healthy dinner three nights in a row—I mainly eat for health during the week, not pleasure.

2. **Off-load your memory with your camera phone.** I have a horrible memory, but I've learned to off-load short-term memory items to my phone. Some of the things I might take pictures of: my hotel room number, where I parked my car, the label from a good bottle of wine, a book cover that a friend shows me, a whiteboard filled with great notes, or the valet parking ticket. It's an easy way to relieve stress and save a

few minutes of wandering around looking for your room or car.

3. **Mute your phone and shut off all notifications.** Working distraction free has already been a theme throughout this book, but it is absolutely crazy to let your computer, phone, or other devices "shout" at you with notifications. My phone is on silent at all times, unless my kids are out at night and I want to make sure I can respond in an emergency. There is no need to be notified every time someone DMs you on Twitter, PMs you on Facebook, or emails you.

4. **Drink a healthy protein shake for breakfast.** Right now, you are probably skipping breakfast to save time, or you are stopping at a Starbucks or Dunkin Donuts to grab coffee and a donut. Both are bad ideas. Remember it's about productivity, not time, and drinking a protein shake gives you energy and alertness all morning, boosting your metabolism so you'll actually burn more calories than if you skip breakfast. And as fast as your dash into a donut shop is, making a shake is faster than parking, walking in, waiting in line, waiting for your coffee, and walking back out.

5. **Never watch live TV.** Why? Because of the commercials. Just DVR every show you want to watch so you can skip through the commercials. Unless it's a real-time sporting event or the Bachelor is giving his final rose, do you really need to watch a TV show the moment it's broadcast?

6. **Don't watch TV at all!** David Meerman Scott is a marketing & sales strategist, keynote speaker, and bestselling author of 10 books including *The New*

Rules of Marketing & PR and *Newsjacking*. In an interview for this book he told me:

According to Nielsen, the average American spends 158 hours each month watching television! That's 1,896 hours per year. Damn. That would be enough time to write an awesome book or start a company. You want a six-pack? Exercise instead of watch TV. Eliminate television and you gain nearly two thousand hours a year. Imagine what YOU could do!

7. **Use your drive time wisely.** Think about how many hours a year you spend driving in the car. Commute times, driving to clients, long trips to your parents' house. Even if you just drive 30 minutes each way to work, that is over 200 hours a year, or almost 10 days of time. We often reflexively just think of this as dead time on our calendar and crank up our favorite music and tune out the world. Instead, think of phone calls you need to make—whether work related or to friends and family members. Consider listening to podcasts (which can cover the daily news) or "how to" programs or even learning a foreign language. Of course you can use podcast apps like Stitcher (www.Stitcher.com) to easily find great programs and listen to them at 2x the speed to save even more time!

8. **Never call people without setting an appointment ahead of time (unless it's social, of course).** How often do you call unannounced and get someone's voicemail? "Hey Jane, just wanted to catch up to hear how the sales meeting went; call me back." And then

Jane calls you, and you're busy so she gets your voicemail, "Hey, it's Jane, just returning your call. Call me back." And on and on, like a voicemail ping pong game. Instead, send a calendar invite or email that just says, "Jane, let's connect on phone so I can get debriefed on sales meeting. Is tomorrow at 11:00 a.m. ET good? If not, suggest a few openings on your day." Notice "a few" so you don't end up with email ping pong trying to find time on each other's calendars.

9. **Avoid busy times out in the real world if at all possible.** This secret will save many minutes a week and many hours in the year. It's as simple as shifting when you do things you have to do. Instead of shopping for groceries on busy Saturday morning, do it late Friday night or early Sunday morning instead. Don't schedule trips to clients close to rush hour drive times. Don't go into the bank during lunch hours.

10. **Use dual monitors.** Adding a second monitor to your computer setup is one of the easiest ways to gain massive efficiency for your computer tasks. It completely eliminates that need to toggle between two different windows. I actually work with one monitor on one computer and two monitors on another computer, so technically I have three monitors going at the same time. But even with just two, you can then easily type in your word processor while reviewing research material on the Internet, preview code in one window while debugging in the other, or if you aren't on a focus sprint, yes you can monitor email traffic or view

your calendar in one window while being constructive in the other.

11. **Have a stop doing list.** The great business thinker Jim Collins has often said that your "stop doing" list is just as important, if not more important, than your to-do list. In his 2003 article (http://www.jimcollins.com/article_topics/articles/best-new-years.html), he talks about how great companies practice this, and he himself uses New Year's resolution time to work on his stop doing list. Simplicity and minimalism can free the mind, free your schedule, and enable you to do great work.

12. **Remind people of the "end time."** There was a time when I reported to the CEO of a large company and had assumed major new responsibilities. I quickly started drowning. My CEO's assistant offered to follow me around to help. At the end of two weeks, she said, "One thing that you need to do is really commit to the end time. Don't let people keep you longer than they were scheduled for." Great advice. Ever since, I start every meeting, and especially every phone call, with, "Before we get started, I see we are scheduled for 30 minutes, and I do have a hard stop 3:00..." This way everyone knows in advance that it won't be a casual, leisurely meeting that just runs its own course. This tip is especially critical if you schedule calls for only 10 or 15 minutes.

13. **Hang out with productive people.** Seems silly, but so powerful. If your best friends at work are the ones taking 90-minute lunches all the time, you're likely to do the same. If your social circle routinely does happy

hour and discusses what happened on reality TV the night before, you're likely to continue doing the same. Consider upgrading your work friends and your other friends. If for some reason you can't find productive time ninjas around you, hang out with them online. I've joined Facebook groups for entrepreneurs, writers, runners, and on and on. It's a great way to "hang" with people who are motivating each other, sharing their productivity tips, and keeping each other on the path to success.

14. **Tell people around you to leave you alone.** As the *Wall Street Journal* reported in their September 11, 2013, edition, the biggest distraction to work isn't email or instant messenger—it's face-to-face interruptions. If you work from home, make it clear to your family that work is work, and they can't interrupt you. If you're in the office, consider hanging a "Do Not Disturb" or "Back at [time]" sign on your door or running yellow caution tape across your cube entrance. And if you're the boss, consider setting aside a couple hours of day throughout the office for quiet time.

15. **Buy birthday cards by the dozen.** Do you go out and buy a card every time a friend or family member's birthday comes up? Or do you rush out to buy a condolence card each time you need one? The next time just go out and buy 10–20 cards—whatever a year's worth is—and a roll of stamps and keep them in your desk drawer so they're ready to go. Think of how many 15-minute trips to the store you will save in a given year.

16. **Pay bills electronically.** Do you pay bills every week or two the old fashioned way, with checks and stamps? Big time waster. Just sign up for automatic bill pay—using a credit card whenever possible so you can earn points. You do need to leave a little extra money in your checking account to make sure you never run short, but it's worth the slight cash inefficiency to save all that time.

17. **Never answer a call from an unknown number.** If they're not in your contact list, it's highly unlikely the call is from a friend, family member, or big client. The odds are high it's a sales call or a friend of a friend who was given your number. And even if the call is from someone you know, it's always best to have call time scheduled on your calendar.

18. **Get a business coach, mentor, or mastermind group.** This may sound unusual as time management advice, but connecting with someone who has already walked the path you're on can save you a lot of time (not to mention money and frustration).

19. **Release your content through multiple channels.** Joe Pulizzi, author of *Epic Content Marketing*, offers this advice, "Plan your content creation in advance. Most people think in content tactics, like publishing a blog or a Facebook post. It's best to think in stories, and how many ways you can tell that story—an article, a blog, a book, a webinar, multiple social media posts, an ebook, a podcast and more. The time savings are immense if you only plan in advance."

20. **Know that done is better than perfect.** Software developers will often say, "Shipped is better than per-

fect." And the release of software version 1.0 is quickly followed by version 1.1, 1.2, and on and on to fix the bugs inevitably contained in the initial release. As a writer it's too easy to keep working on my book...new material, new ideas, better ways of phrasing things. But published imperfectly is of more value to the world than never published at all.

In Their Own Words...

I don't add time to activities. Hell, I wear a different watch each day and I don't even take the time to set them. I get as much done as I can as quickly as I can, waste no time on the little things and if I mess up I will go back and clean it up.

—Grant Cardone is a New York Times bestselling author, sales expert and founder of four companies.

CHAPTER 18

Time Secrets of 7 Billionaires

"Billionaire." Just say the word and you capture people's attention. Seven billion people on the planet, and only 1,645 billionaires (according to *Forbes*).

Do *self-made* billionaires work differently than the rest of us? Do you think they know something about time and productivity that helped them to *become* a billionaire?

I reached out to 28 billionaires, and to my surprise, seven of them responded, albeit with brief messages. This is the same response rate—one in four—that I got from contacting 800 "regular old" millionaires and startup CEOs. Mark Cuban actually responded to my email only 61 minutes after I sent it. (Yes, I counted.)

Although this cohort is small in number, it does seem re-markable that three of the seven billionaires' advice relates to meetings. Whether it's keep your mornings clear of them, ban them from one day each week, or "never do meetings unless someone is writing a check" (Cuban) these highly successful people are mindful of the scourge of meetings.

Other advice tailored for entrepreneurs included a warning against multitasking, the need for self-care and not getting distracted by things that aren't critical to your success.

The time and productivity advice in their own words appears below.

NATHAN BLECHARCZYK is the co-founder of Airbnb. In an interview for this book Nathan referred me to his advice that originally appeared on Lifehacker.com:

> *I try to fill my calendar in reverse, from the end-of-day to earlier; I try to reserve the morning for doing "real work." I find I can focus more in the morning whereas it's harder to get focused after having been bombarded by meetings, so I try to save meetings for later in the day.*

MIKE CANNON-BROOKES is the co-founder of Atlassian, an Australian enterprise software company, with over 35,000 global customers. His productivity advice:

> *Do one thing at once. Stop multitasking!*

MARK CUBAN is the owner of the Dallas Mavericks, Magnolia Pictures, Landmark Theatres, chairman of AXS TV and appears on the TV-show Shark Tank. His productivity advice submitted for this book:

Never do meetings unless someone is writing a check.

MOHAMMED DEWJI is the CEO of Tanzania-based MeTL Group. *Forbes* has called him the youngest billionaire in Africa. In an interview for this book, Mohammed provided this productivity advice:

Making time for yourself is essential to maintaining mental fitness and it goes without saying that mental fitness is inextricably linked to your success. Based on personal experience, I have found that maintaining optimum energy levels and focus becomes increasingly challenging as one embarks on new endeavors and climbs the ranks. Particularly when your day consists of switching gears between sifting through hundreds of emails and attending one meet after another, it's only natural for your eyes to get tired and your brain to slow down as the day progresses.

For me, it's a daily workout during my lunch hour that keeps me sane. On most days, by 1:00 p.m. I have already put in about seven hours of work. At that time, it's a no brainer that I need to recharge and refresh so that I can handle the second half of my day with the same focus and energy as I did the first half. Every person has a different way of staying invigorated and recharging his or her batteries. It doesn't matter what it is, you just have to identify it and make time for it. I

> *would strongly encourage new entrepreneurs to heed*
> *this advice because a fresh mind holds the key to their*
> *success.*

ANDREW MASON is the co-founder of Detour and former co-founder and CEO of Groupon. In an interview for this book, Andrew provided this productivity advice:

> *Rather than give a specific piece of advice (I have tons*
> *but none of it is rocket science), I'll just say that actual-*
> *ly being disciplined about adopting these habits is, in*
> *my experience, a huge differentiator of successful peo-*
> *ple.*
>
> *I often meet people who seem smarter than me yet are*
> *less capable because they don't have the self-discipline*
> *and/or self-confidence to introspect on their ability to*
> *do what they think they're going to do and find ways to*
> *iteratively improve. Amazingly, I think it's as simple as*
> *that. It's kind of a sore spot for me because I can't un-*
> *derstand why more people don't take it seriously.*
>
> *If I was building a character in a business video game*
> *and I had ten character points to distribute I'd put 3 of*
> *them into intelligence and 7 of them into self-discipline.*

DUSTIN MOSKOVITZ is co-founder of the team productivity app Asana (www.Asana.com) and co-founded Facebook. In an interview for this book, Dustin provided this productivity advice:

> *Pick one day a week that you and your team can focus*
> *on getting individual work done without any interrup-*
> *tions like meetings. At Asana, we have No Meeting*

Wednesdays established to encourage flow and productivity across the company.

MARK PINCUS is the co-founder and CEO of Zynga. In an interview for this book, Mark provided this productivity advice

If you want to build great products, devote more than 50 percent of your work hours to product. Don't accept speaking opportunities if you can't justify them as benefitting your users or your company.

Nobody would argue that stellar time management is the key to becoming a billionaire, but the wisdom of those who've quickly climbed to the very peak of business success certainly can accelerate our own progress.

CHAPTER 19

Time Secrets of 13 Olympic Athletes

How do Olympic athletes maintain their focus, discipline and energy? How do the unsponsored athletes juggle their "day job" with their training and family obligations?

Perhaps more than any other group, Olympic athletes are truly working against a ticking clock. Four years in between Olympic Games. Each day that passes takes the athletes closer and closer to their big moment. It's a moment when winning a medal or not can literally come down to fractions of a second.

Similar to the other highly successful people I interviewed, Olympic athletes stressed the importance of scheduling everything on the calendar and having clear priorities.

What was unique to this group was how often they brought up the importance of sleep and the need to rejuvenate. Maximizing energy, not just time, is paramount to athletes.

Gymnast Shannon Miller mentioned, "Grabbing a power nap." Olympic rower, Will Dean, said, "To be at your best, you need some down time. Don't feel bad about napping." Katie Uhlanender, a skeleton racer, advised, "It is important to also schedule time for yourself, to rest, or to refocus." And cyclist, Chris Carmichael, believes "Rest is perhaps the most overlooked and undervalued aspect of time management."

The advice given by all the Olympic athletes I interviewed is below.

SARA HENDERSHOT, an Olympic rower for the United States, competed in the 2012 Olympics. She is currently training for Rio 2016. Her advice:

My philosophy is that when I have the energy and the focus to make decisions like what I want my next day to look like, that is when I have to make those decisions. I will basically plot out what I know a day needs to look like, and how I'm going to work through my to-do list and how much time I'm going to allow myself to spend on each one of these tasks so that when I actually am in that moment getting it done, there are far less decisions to be made.

I use this Moleskine notebook that I'll just carry around with me. I make training notes in it. I make work notes in it. I have a whole bookshelf full of old ones at home, because I'll go back and refer to old things in it all the time.

I don't actually use a calendar; it will be a page in my notebook that I will write...so when I get home at 7:30am, I need to use 7:30 to 8:00 to write this email. Then from 8:00 to 8:15 I need to update this document. That's the kind of plotting that I'll do.

Part of being an Olympic athlete is just that there are a lot of things that I have to miss, and moments or events that I have to skip. I've almost just gotten to the point where I'm used to having to say "No" to things. It's just getting good at knowing your limits and not trying to overstretch those limits because when I do, that's the times that I get injured or I get sick.

SHANNON MILLER, a member of the 1992 and 1996 United States Olympic women's gymnastics team, won a combined seven Olympic medals. She is the most decorated gymnast in American history. Her advice:

During training, I balanced family time, chores, schoolwork, Olympic training, appearances, and other obligations by outlining a very specific schedule. I was forced to prioritize. There were certain things that had to be done at very specific times, like training 7-8am and 3:30-8:30pm. School was 8am-2:30pm. Those times did not waiver. Then I built in everything else around those times giving weight to the most critical to achieving my goal. Most importantly, WRITE IT DOWN. To this day, I keep a schedule that is almost minute by minute. When you do this, you find that there are often pockets of time that you aren't maximizing, for example doing homework on planes and buses. Grabbing a power nap to facilitate recovery instead of wasting an hour online. Focus on those things that bring you further to your goal each and every day. Every moment counts!

WILL DEAN, an Olympic Rower for Canada, competed in the London 2012 Olympics. He is currently training for Rio 2016. His advice:

Get one of those big blue calendars. Planning your life on your phone is fine, but it doesn't give you the same perspective.

Don't feel bad about saying no to people if you're too busy. People will always want your time, and while many things might seem small, they can add up quickly. You have to prioritize your sport and your health, only add to that if it doesn't compromise those two things.

Realize that good time management doesn't mean filling your day with non-stop productivity. To be at your best, you need some down time. Don't feel bad about napping, watching some TV, or going for a walk.

Don't sacrifice your sleep. Sooner or later, it will catch up with you. You won't perform at your best, and you will get sick.

BRIANA SCURRY won two gold medals as the starting goalkeeper for the United States women's soccer team in 1996 and 2004. Her advice:

Focus is absolutely essential to achieving anything worthwhile. At the highest levels of achievement whether it be athletic, academic, or business one must have white hot, obsessiveness and the belief that no matter what, the objective will be achieved. All great achievement in our society was realized in this essence.

About 6 months before an Olympics, I would relate all the decisions I made to the ultimate vision of winning gold. The simple question I would ask several times a day was "Will this activity help me perform better and therefore help us win gold?"

This question guided me in the right direction. Even if the activity was taking the day off or stepping back for a bit to get better perspective, being mindful of that vision helped me choose the best course of action in order to achieve the goal. It became clear to me the right decision to make and in turn provided sharper focus and made it easier to be disciplined.

ROY-ALLAN BURCH, an Olympic swimmer for Bermuda, competed in the 2008 and 2012 games. He is currently training for Rio 2016. His advice:

A strong discipline is required to reach the pinnacle of our sport. Each day is dedicated toward a vigorous amount of training and when not training, it's important to maximize recovery for the next workout...Having a detailed schedule to follow makes maximizing each day easier. Rather than thinking about what needs to happen in an allotted time, one can just execute the training or recovery that needs to take place. As there are thousands of athletes around the world training very hard, time maximization becomes the main race. The question of who can get in the best work for themselves each day becomes a major factor to the success of each individual athlete.

KATIE UHLAENDER, an Olympic skeleton racer for the United States, competed in the Olympics in 2006, 2010 and 2014. Her advice:

One of the most important parts to managing your time well is having an agenda, meaning you have a focus each day and a goal each week. When you are an athlete and constantly training and competing, rest is incredibly important so that you are able to be at your very best physically and mentally. It is important to also schedule time for yourself, to rest, or to refocus.

Also, when you are in a competitive sport you have to be able to adapt and overcome the obstacles you face. At the end of the day it's how well you accomplish the process as a whole, not the long term goal, and how adaptable you are to change because processes evolves and is never perfect. The key to discipline is striving for perfection but understanding perfect isn't attainable. To strive for it means you're willing to learn and overcome challenges; therefore creating solutions. It's a day-by-day process and if you walk in the light and focus on each step, you can see the imprint your footstep makes.

ANDREW WEIBRECHT, an Olympic skier for the United States, won a bronze medal in 2010, and the silver medal in the 2014 Olympics. His advice:

To me it has more to do with sacrifice and taking advantage of opportunity when opportunity is presented than management in a sense. The sport that I do is so all consuming in terms of travel and commitment that when I am training and competing that is all I focus on, and when I am off sport I am totally detached. It is more about productive compartmentalizing and making the most of the moment whether that is time off/rest or sport.

ERIN HAMLIN, an Olympic luger for the United States, competed in the 2006 and 2010 Olympics, and won a bronze medal in 2014. Her advice:

> *When it comes to training, I guess I have just always prioritized it so it was easy to make time for. It has also allowed me to put other things off because training is more important at the time.*

CHRIS CARMICHAEL, a cyclist for the United States, competed in the 1984 Olympics. His advice:

> *Rest is perhaps the most overlooked and undervalued aspect of time management. In training we have to teach athletes to focus on prioritizing quality over quantity, and to achieve higher training quality an athlete has to be properly rested and recovered between hard efforts. Rest, therefore, becomes part of training rather than the absence of training.*

TOBY JENKINS, a water polo player for Australia, competed in the 2004 Olympics. Today he is CEO of Bluewire Media, a web strategy and digital marketing firm. His advice:

> *Find someone whose work you trust and admire and who has already done specifically what you want to do. Ask them for help and then filter their advice for your own situation. It's not about saving an hour or there. It's about saving you potentially years to get to goal.*
>
> *I had some great water polo coaches throughout my career. Each had strengths and weaknesses. My realization though, was that if I had a specific challenge, then I needed a specific answer.*
>
> *When I wanted to put on muscle, I didn't speak to my water polo coach. I spoke to my strength coach, a discus and shot put guy who had put on more weight, faster than anyone else I knew.*

When I was nervous before games, I'd speak to my captain who'd played hundreds of internationals and learn from his pre-game routines.

When I wanted to improve my swimming speed and endurance, I went to a swimming coach who was coaching some of Australia's fastest swimmers at the time.

It all seems pretty obvious but being specific about the challenge you face and then finding the specific person best in a position to help you accelerated my learning enormously. It would be nearly impossible to quantify how many hours this saved me over my career as an athlete, student and now in business.

JULIE MCDONALD, a long-distance freestyle swimmer for Australia, won a bronze medal at the 1988 Olympics. Her advice:

For me, it's about scheduling my time. If I don't schedule my time I get distracted and am not productive. So I allocate time for exercise, charity, work and fun! That way I stay organised.

SCOTT DANBERG has appeared in five Paralympics representing America in track and field, swimming and powerlifting. He is a Fitness Director at the Pritikin Longevity Center. His advice:

As a 5-time Paralympian, a way I have found successful to balance sport training and "life" is to envision my training demands and the multiple responsibilities and obligations of "life" and place it all on an imaginary shelf. Mind you, it's a long shelf with multiple, moveable, dividers that I can compartmentalize and prioritize tasks and change their distribution over time. Tasks such as work and school have fixed dividers of time as these are responsibilities that have known hours and days and need to be met for one's livelihood and future. Other tasks, such as family and leisure pursuits, have flexible dividers of time that although occupy a "somewhat" fixed area on the shelf are flexible in the hours and days or blocks of time in which they occur. Likewise, training for sport also has dividers that are "somewhat" fixed but most also remain flexible, most importantly, to balance against family and leisure pursuits. As much as one may believe they need to "live and breathe" their sport, life balance, specifically interests outside of the sport itself, is as important a quality for athletic success as the sport training itself.

Once the "shelf" is initially organized it doesn't stay that way for long as the priority and time demands of sport training increase as the competitive season and competition nears. The fixed areas on the shelf generally stay the same, so it's the flexible areas on the shelf that change. Unfortunately, an athlete has to cut into time for family and/or leisure pursuits in order to train to be competitive. It's the unfortunate life of an athlete who, at times, spends less time with family and leisure, but the family who is supportive of this, in return, greatly aids in the success of the athlete. The athlete is willing to sacrifice family and leisure time to stay focused on training as it is the passion and drive to be athletically successful that justifies the compromise.

VINCE POSCENTE, a speed skier for Canada, competed in the 1992 Olympics. Today he is CEO of Big Goals Fast Institute, and the *New York Times* bestselling author of *The Age of Speed*. His advice:

Start every day listing off your five MITs (Most Important Things) and get those done first.

The biggest time waster, especially in a competitive landscape is to try to do it all. The heroes of sport are the ones who spend extra time in the gym or the batting cage or at the rink. But they can be more efficient. What got me to the Olympics was doing what the competition was not willing to do. These weren't necessarily big things. Examples include: read books on aerodynamics, learn how skis were made, interview a PhD in the politics of sport, use visualization and imagery over two hours per day with bio feedback, sensory deprivation float tanks, hypnosis programs, meditation and read a cutting-edge book on mental training every three weeks.

Although you might not be training for the 2016 Rio games, you are definitely in competition as you fight to achieve your goals. How will these time and productivity tips get *you* closer to the finish line?

CHAPTER 20

Time Secrets of 29 Straight-A Students

What does it take to maintain straight A's at MIT or Harvard?

What does it take to be a straight-A student in high school, while juggling varsity sports and numerous activities? The students I interviewed gave a wide range of advice and there are too many responses to include verbatim in this book. The word cloud image below summarizes their responses.

I'm reminded in my own home that there is no one way to achieve productivity and success as a student. My two teenage daughters are both straight-A students, yet they have very different study habits. One listens to music while studying, the other doesn't. One checks social media as her "reward" for getting a piece of homework done, while the other leaves her phone in a different room to avoid the temptation.

What was most unique in this group of high achievers was how often they talked about social media. Almost everyone mentioned the siren call of Snapchat, Instagram or Facebook, and many suggested specific apps as a way to manage those urges (e.g., SelfControl, StayFocused).

In addition to the familiar advice about using a calendar and being clear on priorities, straight-A students also know how to say no. From having no social life, or limiting friends to study groups, these suggestions—while seemingly extreme—might be the price to pay for excelling at the highest levels in academics.

CHAPTER 21

Time Secrets of 239 Entrepreneurs

Innovators, risk takers, dream chasers, business moguls, self-made millionaires…in other words, *entrepreneurs*. Arguably no other group feels the pressure of multiple obligations. Most are overseeing sales as well as product development. Customer service and raising capital. Podcasting, writing books, speaking at conferences. How do entrepreneurs manage to be so productive?

I collected over 25,000 words from entrepreneurs in response to my questions about time management and productivity. Too many responses to include verbatim in this book.

With such diversity in people and answers there is of course no one consistent answer to increasing productivity. However, as the answers started coming back what did surprise me was how many entrepreneurs brought up the importance of a morning routine. These responses were totally unaided—I didn't ask about their routine, or if they had one, and was actually startled by how many brought it up.

Other themes that emerged included the importance of scheduling everything you want to accomplish on your calendar, the dangers of unmanaged email, and the need for focus. No multi-tasking for this group.

Quiz: Discover Your Time Management Personality

The Time Management Style Assessment (TMSA), by Kevin Kruse, will give you a thorough analysis of your current time management behaviors. The two primary factors driving time mastery are being clear on your priorities, and using the mechanics of planning (based on the groundbreaking 1994 research of Dr. Therese Hoff Macan). Understanding your current level of competence in these two domains will enable you to identify areas for improvement and further productivity gains.

Take the quiz and get your custom report at:

www.KevinKruse.com/time

110 Best Time Management Quotes

1. Yesterday is history. Tomorrow is a mystery. Today is a gift. That's why it's called the present. – **Eleanor Roosevelt**

2. Don't wait. The time will never be just right. – **Napoleon Hill**

3. A day wasted on others is not wasted on one's self. – **Charles Dickens**

4. A man who dares to waste one hour of life has not discovered the value of life. – **Charles Darwin**

5. A wise person does at once what a fool does at last. Both do the same thing; only at different times. – **Baltasar Gracián**

6. Live each day as if it be your last. – **Marcus Aurelius**

7. All great achievements require time. – **Maya Angelou**

8. All that really belongs to us is time; even he who has nothing else has that. – **Baltasar Gracián**

9. All the flowers of all of the tomorrows are in the seeds of today. – **Chinese Proverb**

10. All the forces in the world are not so powerful as an idea whose time has come. – **Victor Hugo**

11. Be mindful of how you approach time. Watching the clock is not the same as watching the sun rise. – **Sophia Bedford-Pierce**

12. Believe that time is going to help you do what you want. – **William Morris Hunt**

13. Better three hours too soon than one minute too late. – **William Shakespeare**

14. Clock watchers never seem to be having a good time. – **James Cash Penney**

15. Determine never to be idle. No person will have occasion to complain of the want of time who never loses any. It is wonderful how much can be done if we are always doing. – **Thomas Jefferson**

16. Do not confuse motion and progress. A rocking horse keeps moving but does not make any progress. – **Alfred A. Montapert**

17. Do not dwell in the past, do not dream of the future, concentrate the mind on the present moment. – **Buddha**

18. Don't be fooled by the calendar. There are only as many days in the year as you make use of. One man gets only a week's value out of a year while another man gets a full year's value out of a week. – **Charles Richards**

19. Don't be stomping on ants when you have elephants to feed. – **Peter Turla**

20. Don't let the fear of the time it will take to accomplish something stand in the way of your doing it. The time will pass anyway; we might just as well put that passing time to the best possible use. – **Earl Nightingale**

21. Don't say you don't have enough time. You have exactly the same number of hours per day that were given to Helen Keller, Pasteur, Michelangelo, Mother Teresa, Leonardo da Vinci, Thomas Jefferson, and Albert Einstein. – **H. Jackson Brown**

22. Don't spend a dollar's worth of time on a ten-cent decision. – **Peter Turla**

23. Dost thou love life? Then do not squander time, for that's the stuff that life is made of. – **Benjamin Franklin**

24. Even if you're on the right track, you'll get run over if you just sit there. – **Will Rogers**

25. Nothing else, perhaps, distinguishes effective executives as much as their tender loving care of time. – **Peter Drucker**

26. For time and the world do not stand still. Change is the law of life. And those who look only to the past or the present are certain to miss the future. – **John F. Kennedy**

27. Gaining time is gaining everything in love, trade and war. – **John Shebbeare**

28. Half our life is spent trying to find something to do with the time we have rushed through life trying to save. – **Will Rogers**

29. I made this letter longer than usual because I lack the time to make it shorter. – **Pascal**

30. He does not seem to me to be a free man who does not sometimes do nothing. – **Cicero**

31. He lives long that lives well; and time misspent is not lived but lost. – **Thomas Fuller**

32. He that rises late must trot all day. – **Benjamin Franklin**

33. He who gains time gains everything. – **Benjamin Disraeli**

34. He who knows most grieves most for wasted time.–**Dante**

35. I don't think of the past. The only thing that matters is the everlasting present. – **Somerset Maugham**

36. I recommend to you to take care of the minutes; for hours will take care of themselves. – **Lord Chesterfield**

37. I'm too busy mopping the floor to turn off the faucet. – **Unknown**

38. If it weren't for the last minute, a lot of things wouldn't get done. – **Michael S. Traylor**

39. If you want to make good use of your time, you've got to know what's most important and then give it all you've got. – **Lee Iacocca**

40. In the real world, nothing happens at the right place at the right time. It is the job of journalists and historians to correct that. – **Mark Twain**

41. In truth, people can generally make time for what they choose to do; it is not really the time but the will that is lacking. – **Sir John Lubbock**

42. It is a mistake to look too far ahead. Only one link of the chain of destiny can be handled at a time. – **Winston Churchill**

43. It is better to have lived one day as a tiger than a thousand years as a sheep. – **Tibetan saying**

44. It's better to do the right thing slowly than the wrong thing quickly. – **Peter Turla**

45. It's how we spend our time here and now that really matters. If you are fed up with the way you have come to interact with time, change it. – **Marcia Wieder**

46. It's not enough to be busy, so are the ants. The question is, what are we busy about? – **Henry David Thoreau**

47. Know the true value of time; snatch, seize, and enjoy every moment of it. No idleness, no laziness, no procrastination; never put off till tomorrow what you can do today. – **Lord Chesterfield**

48. Lost time is never found again. – **Proverb**

49. Never leave till tomorrow that which you can do today. – **Benjamin Franklin**

50. Lost wealth may be replaced by industry, lost knowledge by study, lost health by temperance or medicine, but lost time is gone forever. – **Samuel Smiles**

51. Make use of time, let not advantage slip. – **William Shakespeare**

52. Managing your time without setting priorities is like shooting randomly and calling whatever you hit the target. – **Peter Turla**

53. Many people take no care of their money till they come nearly to the end of it, and others do just the same with their time. – **Goethe**

54. Money is a wonderful thing, but it is possible to pay too high a price for it. – **Alexander Bloch**

55. Money, I can only gain or lose. But time I can only lose. So, I must spend it carefully. –**Unknown**

56. Never let yesterday use up today. – **Richard H. Nelson**

57. Nothing is a waste of time if you use the experience wisely. – **Rodin**

58. Nothing is ours except Time. – **Goethe**

59. Once you have mastered time, you will understand how true it is that most people overestimate what they can accomplish in a year—and underestimate what they can achieve in a decade! – **Anthony Robbins**

60. One always has time enough, if one will apply it well. –**Goethe**

61. One worthwhile task carried to a successful conclusion is worth half-a-hundred half-finished tasks. – **Malcolm Forbes**

62. Ordinary people think merely of spending time. Great people think of using it. –**Unknown**

63. Realize that now, in this moment of time, you are creating. You are creating your next moment. That is what's real. – **Sara Paddison**

64. Take a rest. A field that has rested yields a beautiful crop. – **Ovid**

65. Take care of the minutes, and the hours will take care of themselves. – **Lord Chesterfield**

66. The bad news is time flies. The good news is you're the pilot. – **Michael Altshuler**

67. The great dividing line between success and failure can be expressed in five words: "I did not have time." – **Franklin Field**

68. The key is in not spending time, but in investing it. – **Stephen R. Covey**

69. The most important question to ask is, what am I becoming? – **Jim Rohn**

70. The surest way to be late is to have plenty of time. – **Leo Kennedy**

71. The time for action is now. It's never too late to do something. – **Carl Sandburg**

72. The time you enjoy wasting is not wasted time. – **Bertrand Russell**

73. The worst days of those who enjoy what they do are better than the best days of those who don't. – **Jim Rohn**

74. There is nothing so useless as doing efficiently that which should not be done at all. – **Peter Drucker**

75. This time, like all times, is a very good one, if we but know what to do with it. – **Ralph Waldo Emerson**

76. Those who make the worst use of their time are the first to complain of its shortness. – **Jean De La Bruyere**

77. Time and I against any two. – **Baltasar Gracian**

78. Time and the hour run through the roughest day. – **William Shakespeare**

79. Time as he grows old teaches many lessons. – **Aeschylus**

80. Time is a great healer, but a poor beautician. – **Lucille Harper**

81. Time is a great teacher, but unfortunately it kills all its pupils. – **Hector Louis Berlioz**

82. Time is at once the most valuable and the most perishable of all our possessions. – **John Randolph**

83. Time is money. – **Benjamin Franklin**

84. Time is really the only capital that any human being has, and the only thing he can't afford to lose. – **Thomas Edison**

85. Time is the coin of your life. It is the only coin you have, and only you can determine how it will be spent. Be careful lest you let other people spend it for you. – **Carl Sandburg**

86. Time is the rider that breaks youth. – **George Herbert**

87. Time is the school in which we learn, time is the fire in which we burn. – **Delmore Schwartz**

88. Time is the wisest counselor of all. – **Pericles**

89. Time is what we want most, but what we use worst. – **William Penn**

90. Time lost is never found again. – **Benjamin Franklin**

91. Time makes heroes but dissolves celebrities. – **Daniel J. Boorstin**

92. Time stays long enough for those who use it. – **Leonardo Da Vinci**

93. Time will take your money, but money won't buy time. – **James Taylor**

94. To do two things at once is to do neither. – **Publius Syrus**

95. To think too long about doing a thing often becomes its undoing. – **Eva Young**

96. Until we can manage time, we can manage nothing else. – **Peter Drucker**

97. Until you value yourself, you will not value your time. Until you value your time, you will not do anything with it. – **M. Scott Peck**

98. We can no more afford to spend major time on minor things than we can to spend minor time on major things. – **Jim Rohn**

99. What may be done at any time will be done at no time. – **Scottish Proverb**

100. When I am getting ready to reason with a man, I spend one-third of my time thinking about myself and what I am going to say and two-thirds about him and what he is going to say. – **Abraham Lincoln**

101. Whether it's the best of times or the worst of times, it's the only time we've got. – **Art Buchwald**

102. While we are postponing, life speeds by. – **Seneca**

103. Work expands so as to fill the time available for its completion. – **Cyril Parkinson**

104. You can't change the past, but you can ruin the present by worrying about the future. – **Unknown**

105. You cannot do a kindness too soon, for you never know how soon it will be too late. – **Ralph Waldo Emerson**

106. You cannot kill time without injuring eternity. – **Henry David Thoreau**

107. You may delay, but time will not.– **Benjamin Franklin**

108. You must get good at one of two things. Planting in the spring or begging in the fall. – **Jim Rohn**

109. You will never find time for anything. If you want time you must make it. – **Charles Buxton**

110. You've got to think about big things while you're doing small things, so that all the small things go in the right direction. – **Alvin Toffler**

Join the #1440 Movement

Did you learn at least one thing in this book that will make you more productive and give you more time for yourself? If so, please help me to spread the word!

Please share your time and productivity thoughts, notes or questions on Twitter, Facebook and Instagram using the hashtag #1440 (remember, only 1,440 minutes in a day). And search #1440 to see what other people are talking about.

Other ways to help people take back their lives:

1. Share this book with friends who are "overworked and overwhelmed"
2. Buy copies of this book for your employees
3. Recommend this book to your book club
4. Recommend Kevin Kruse to speak at your next corporate event or conference

Extreme Productivity
Workshop or Keynote

Imagine dramatically improving productivity in your organization, while also improving work-life balance!

Extreme Productivity with Kevin Kruse

Kevin Kruse speaks around the world at executive retreats, leadership meetings and association conferences. Based on his bestselling book, *15 Secrets Successful People Know About Time Management*, and on his interviews with hundreds of top achievers, Kevin shares the surprising ways everyone can achieve extreme productivity and stop feeling "overworked and overwhelmed."

To invite Kevin to speak at your next event
email info@kevinkruse.com
Or call 267-756-7089

Kevin Kruse

Kevin Kruse is a *New York Times* bestselling author, *Forbes* contributor, keynote speaker and founder of several multi-million dollar companies. He has advised Fortune 500 CEOs, Marine Corps generals and members of Congress.

In pursuit of the American Dream, Kevin started his first company when he was just 22 years old. He worked around the clock, living out of his one-room office and showering each day at the YMCA, before giving up a year later deeply in debt. But after discovering the power of Wholehearted Leadership and how to "Master Your Minutes", Kevin went on to build and sell several successful companies, winning *Inc* 500 and Best Place to Work awards along the way.

Website: www.KevinKruse.com
LinkedIn: www.linkedin.com/in/kevinkruse67
Facebook: www.facebook.com/KruseAuthor
Twitter: @Kruse
Instagram: kevin__kruse

This book contains articles that were previously published as part of the author's blog on kevinkruse.com, Forbes.com, or other online forums, but have been revised and updated since the date of their original publication.

ISBN-13: 978-0-9850564-3-8
eISBN-13: 978-0-9850564-4-5

Made in the USA
Middletown, DE
31 August 2018